AMELIA SAINT GEORGE'S
KITCHEN STENCIL KIT

AMELIA SAINT GEORGE'S
KITCHEN STENCIL KIT

INCLUDES 8 PULL-OUT STENCILS

EBURY PRESS
LONDON

FOR MY SON
Thomas Jolyon

First published in 1996

1 3 5 7 9 10 8 6 4 2

Text copyright © 1996 Amelia Saint George
Photography copyright © 1996 Ebury Press

The right of Amelia Saint George to be identified as the author of this book has been asserted by her in accordance with the Copyright, Designs and Patents Act 1988.

All rights reserved. No part of this publication may be reproduced, stored in a retrieval system, or transmitted in any form or by any means, electronic, mechanical, photocopying, recording or otherwise, without the prior permission of the copyright owners.

First published in the United Kingdom in 1996 by
Ebury Press, Random House,
20 Vauxhall Bridge Road, London SW1V 2SA

Random House Australia (Pty) Limited,
20 Alfred Street, Milsons Point,
Sydney, New South Wales, 2061, Australia

Random House New Zealand Limited,
18 Poland Road,
Glenfield, Auckland 10, New Zealand

Random House South Africa (Pty) Limited,
PO Box 337,
Bergvlei, South Africa

Random House UK Limited Reg. No. 954009

A catalogue record for this book is available from the British Library

ISBN 0 09 180813 8

Edited by Emma Callery
Designed by Paul Wood
Photographed by John Freeman, except for photographs on pages
3, 13, 14, 15, 16, 17, 27, 28, 29, 30 by Julie Fisher

Colour separations by Digital Imaging (UK) Limited
Printed and bound in Singapore by Tien Wah Press

Contents

INTRODUCTION 6

Fruits and berries 12
Grapevine 18
Trailing acanthus leaves 26

THE PULL-OUT STENCILS 33

Vegetables and herbs 49
Blue flowers 54
Kitchen cutlery 60
Delftware tiles 68
Provençal sunflowers 74

ACKNOWLEDGMENTS 80

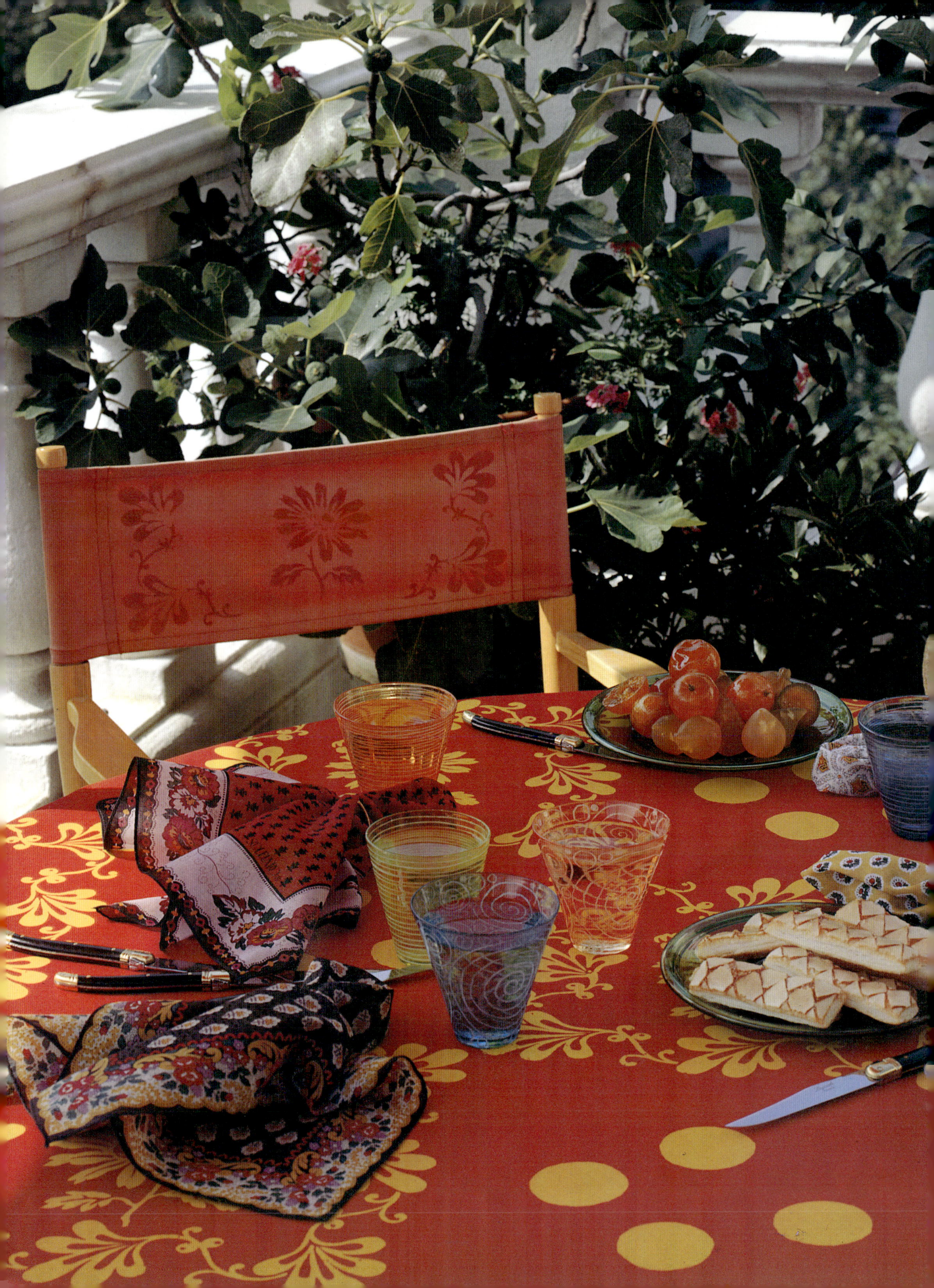

Introduction

When I first approached this book, I found it difficult to think of many ideas. However, after considering all the things that I did in the kitchen, where I did them, and what I used, I quickly realized that there are plenty of subjects to cover. As well as the larger surfaces in a kitchen like walls, floors, cupboards and curtains, there are many other items that can be successfully stencilled, including utensils, tea towels, jar labels, aprons, tablecloths and napkins – you name it, it can be stencilled on. So I set to and developed many new designs specifically with these items in mind, and the end result is this book with its wide range of stencils and colourful kitchens.

My kitchen is used more than any other area in my home. It ranges from being a room for a humble snack, to a place where all the laundry is done, or is the location for one of my grander efforts to entertain a gathering of friends. Because stencils are so easy to use I find that with a small template, a pot of paint and a paintbrush, a kitchen can be quickly transformed. Bright berries used for decorating labels, trailing ivy on cupboard doors, delicate swags of flowers traversing blinds, herbs and vegetables drying on a tablecloth, and strong colours stencilled onto a parasol, are all ideas found within these pages.

So whether you choose to stencil a few presents for friends or totally refurbish your kitchen, this book is an indispensable guide and source of ideas. All the stencils shown in the photographs are provided within the book; many are incorporated ready to cut out and use straight away, and others can quickly be transferred to acetate or oiled manilla paper. Read pages 10-11 for how to use this book and then have a go – stencilling is both easy and, best of all, fun.

Overleaf : The stencil subjects are wide and varied in this book, here are but eight details taken from them. Looking at the tea towels from left to right, they are taken from: Blue Flowers (pages 54-59), Vegetables and Herbs (pages 49-53), Fruits and Berries (pages 12-17), Vegetables and Herbs again, Fruits and Berries again, Blue Flowers again, Grapevine (pages 18-25), and Provençal Sunflowers (pages 74-79).

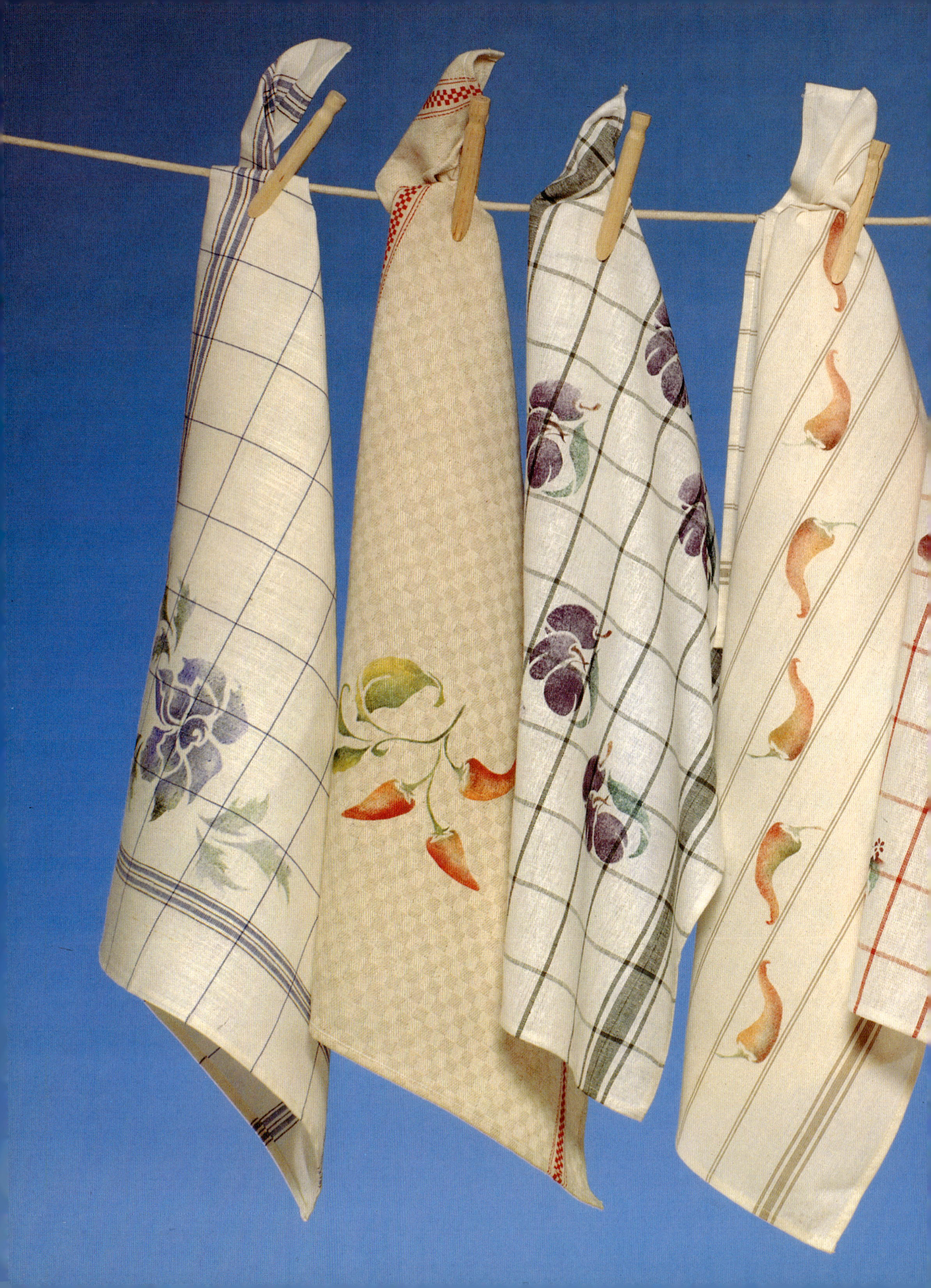

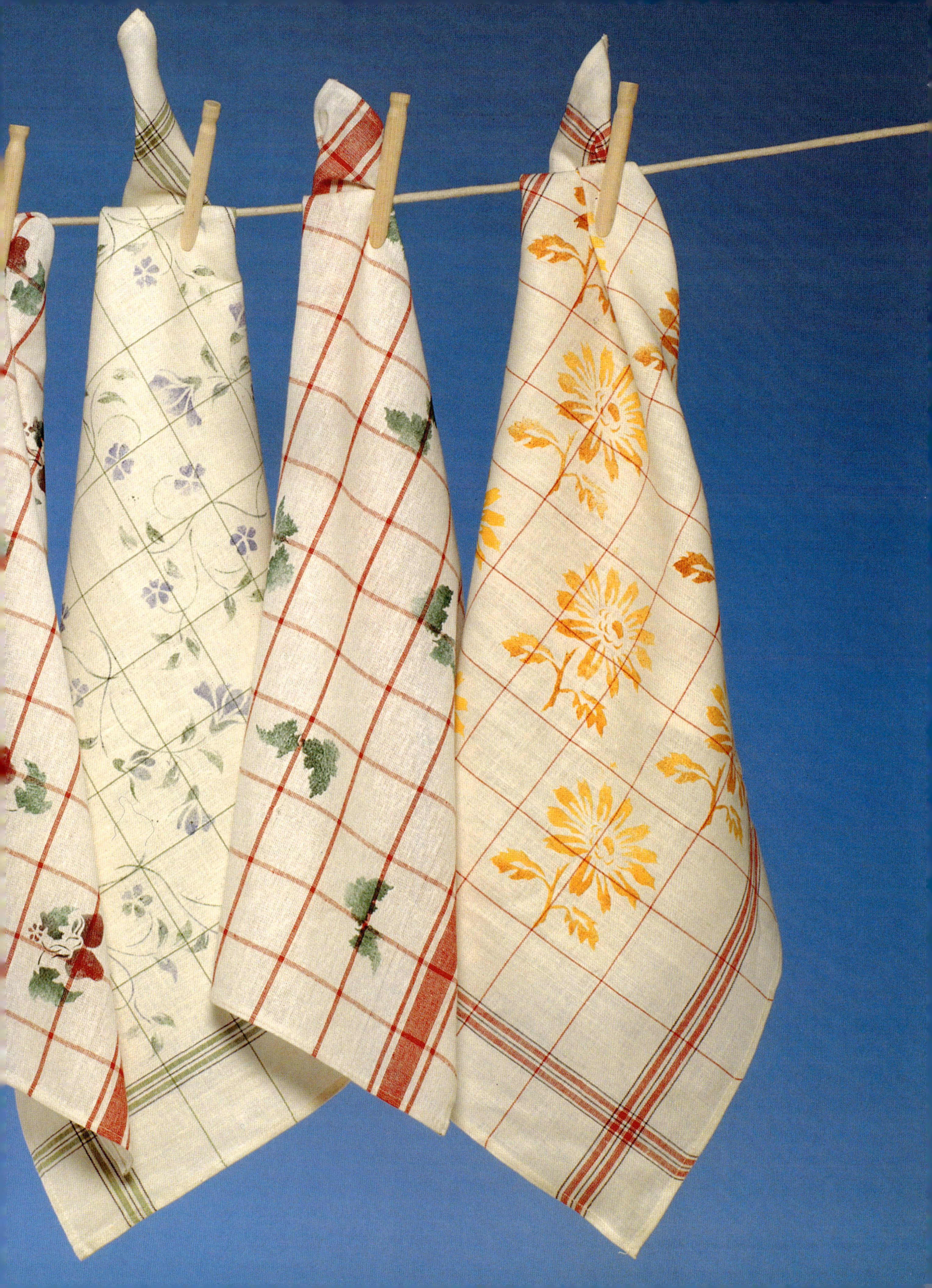

INTRODUCTION

MATERIALS AND EQUIPMENT

CRAFT KNIFE
This is essential for cutting out your stencils, whether you are using a pull-out from the middle of this book, acetate or oiled manilla board. The blade needs to be sharp and clean and do remember that you should always pull the blade away from your body. One slip could cause a terrible injury. For very fiddly designs, you might find a small pair of embroidery scissors useful.

CUTTING MAT
With a good cutting mat beneath your stencil, the cutting out will be made much easier. It will give you a firm and smooth surface on which to lean and will also ensure that you don't cut through onto the work surface by mistake. Use either a PVC self-healing cutting mat which are available in various sizes from any good craft shop, or use a piece of glass sheeting the edges of which have been covered with masking tape for safety.

MASKING TAPE
This is the self-adhesive tape that tears like paper and can be re-used several times before its stick wears out. It is invaluable for stencilling as it can be used when cutting out the stencil, for positioning it on the surface to be stencilled, and also for masking out areas of the design that you might not wish to use.

Not a lot of material is needed for stencilling - a craft knife, cutting mat and piece of acetate or manilla paper (as shown here) to prepare the stencil and then masking tape, paints and a few stencil brushes are all the items that are required.

PAINTS
The chart opposite shows exactly which paints can be used on which surfaces. Acrylic and fabric paints are washable with water, but spray paint needs a solvent like turpentine; the can will tell you exactly which solvent is best to use.

REPOSITIONABLE SPRAY GLUE
Spray glue is a very useful way of sticking a stencil in place before painting through it. It has such a good contact that no paint will slip under the edges of the design. This is particularly useful for spray paints as the force of paint coming from the can can easily cause seepage.

STENCIL BOARDS
The stencils produced on this book are on heavy-duty tracing paper which is durable enough for up to ten or so repeats. If you want to make your own stencils, use either acetate or oiled manilla board, available from craft shops. Descriptions for using these are given later in this book; they are both easy to use and last for as long as you wish to keep the stencil.

STENCIL BRUSHES
For stippling paint, it is best to use stencil brushes as their stubby, stiff bristles allow you to dab on the paint vertically with a repeated, jabbing motion (see page 15). It is best to have as many stencil brushes as you can afford as you can then change your colours far more easily without having to wash out the brush each time. To make sure that your brushes last forever, always clean them thoroughly before putting them away. Use either water or the solvent advised by the manufacturer.

VARNISHES
You might not choose to apply a coat of varnish on top of all your stencils, but several coats of polyurethane varnish in either gloss or matt will protect any stencil that may come up against wear and tear in the kitchen.

INTRODUCTION

HOW TO USE THE BOOK

There are eight different design themes in this book and each one either has a pull-out stencil in the central section or a stencil design included with the chapter. These particular ones can be traced over and used by cutting out the stencil from acetate or manilla paper (see pages 14-15 and 20-1). For the pull-out section, simply pull or cut out the required page and prepare the stencil as described on pages 14-15.

The first three chapters in the book are detailed projects in their own right but at the same time each focuses on particular stencilling techniques. These are:

Pages 14-15
Cutting a stencil
Positioning a stencil
Using acrylic paints

Pages 20-1
Sizing a stencil

Adapting a stencil
Using oiled manilla paper

Pages 28-9
Turning corners
Using spray paints

Whether you are a first-time stenciller or have done it before there is information on these pages that will inform you and develop your technique. So read on.

WHICH PAINT FOR WHICH SURFACE?

	ACRYLIC PAINT	SPRAY CAN	FABRIC
KITCHEN UNITS			
wood	*	*	
melamine		*	
KITCHEN FLOORS			
wood	*	*	
cork tiles	*	*	
rush matting			*
ceramic tiles		* †	*
KITCHEN WALLS	*	*	
OTHER SURFACES			
fabrics			* ††
glass	*	*	
metal containers		*	
plastics †††	*	*	
paper	*	*	

† temporary effect only, no paint is durable on ceramics
†† must be fully washable
††† plastics can be difficult to stencil on so test the bottom first

FRUITS AND BERRIES

Colourful, shapely and easy to combine, fruits and berries are a natural theme for stencil designs. I find that seasonal stencils incorporating these motifs – summer fruits for those hot, languorous days, ivy leaves with berries for the autumn, and mistletoe for Christmas – are very popular, so here are a few for you to try out.

The stencil featured on page 33 is a veritable cornucopia of fruits and berries; there are peaches, plums, redcurrants, strawberries and alpine strawberries, and all their attendant leaves, flowing in abundance across the page. I designed it specifically so that individual elements could be used in addition to the whole stencil. It really is ideal for making small jam jar labels and covers, or for decorating ceramicware – and if you should display your jugs and plates on an open set of shelves, perhaps you could consider stencilling the entire design along the back or around the edge in a softly twisting trail. Alternatively, use the stencil to twist around plates and bowls, or position the stencils so that they appear in spaces between them. As for using elements of the stencil, jam jar covers are ideal. They are also a very neat way of finishing off any jar and are incredibly easy to make. Cut squares or rounds of linen about 2.5cm (1in) wider than the tops and then stencil on the motifs of your choice. To fix the fabric paints in place, iron on the reverse side of the linen with a medium heat. If you don't do this, the first time you come to wash the tops, the paint will wash off too. Once fixed, all you need to do then is tie the tops in place with coloured cotton or string.

Stencils with many elements to the design can be used in all sorts of ways. Here you can see stencilling onto ceramics, napkins, jam jar covers and labels.

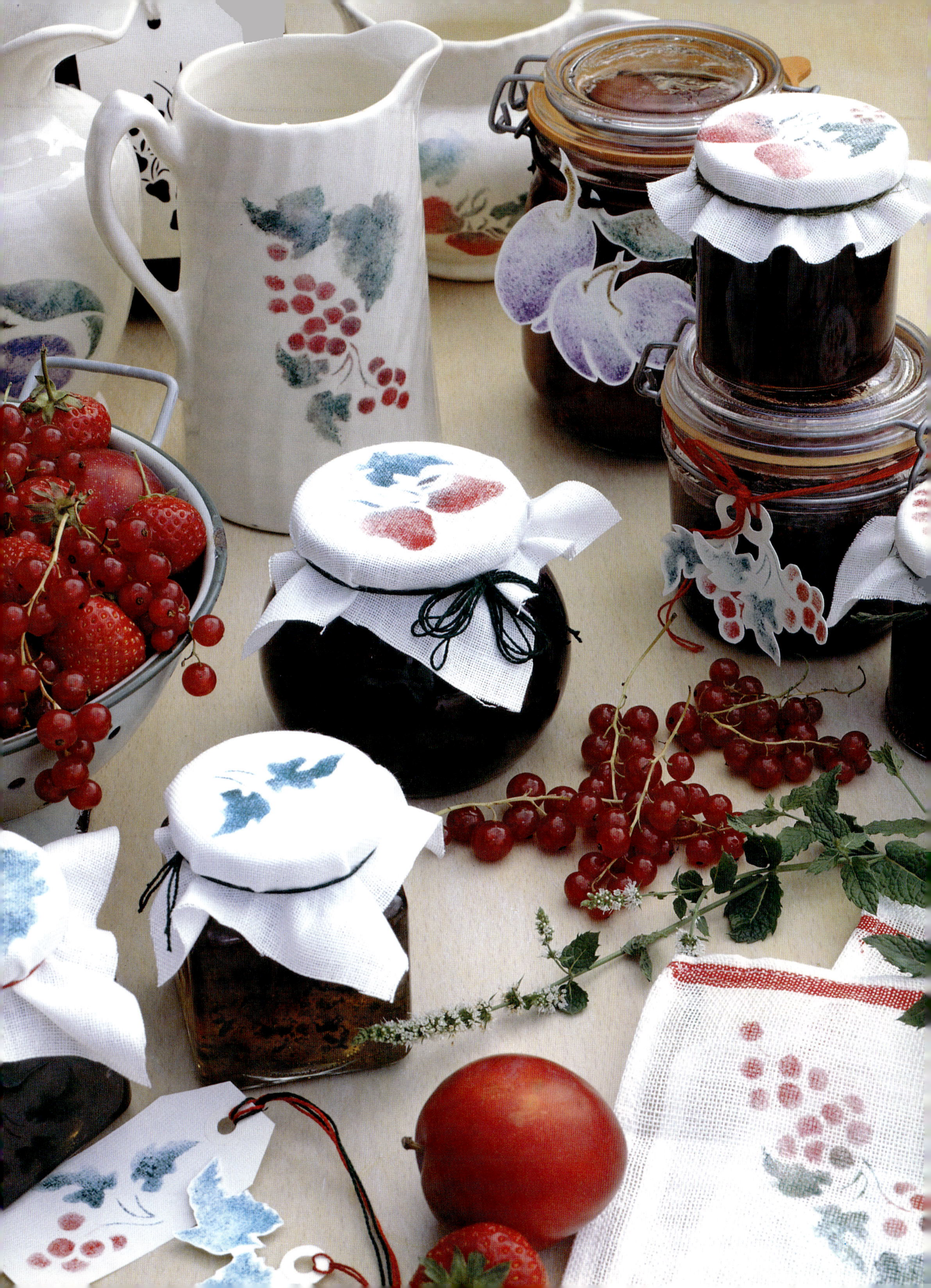

FRUITS AND BERRIES

CUTTING AND POSITIONING A STENCIL AND USING ACRYLIC PAINTS

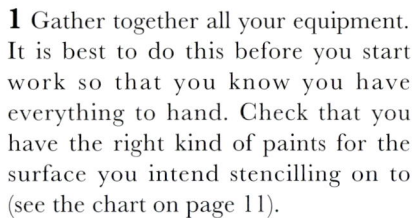

1 Gather together all your equipment. It is best to do this before you start work so that you know you have everything to hand. Check that you have the right kind of paints for the surface you intend stencilling on to (see the chart on page 11).

YOU WILL NEED
Fruits and berries pull-out stencil (see page 33)
Cutting mat
Masking tape
Craft knife or small embroidery scissors
Repositionable spray glue (optional)
Paints
Stencil brushes

2 Cut out the stencil. To do this, fix the stencil paper to a cutting board or mat using strips of masking tape. Then draw the blade gently towards you ensuring your supporting hand is away from the blade. Try not to remove the blade until you have finished cutting out each shape. If you should make a mistake and accidentally cut through a bridge – the areas separating each element of the design – I find they are easily reparable with small strips of masking tape. At this stage you may choose only to cut out part of the stencil, say if you are stencilling just the strawberries onto a label, or you could cut out the whole design.

FRUITS AND BERRIES

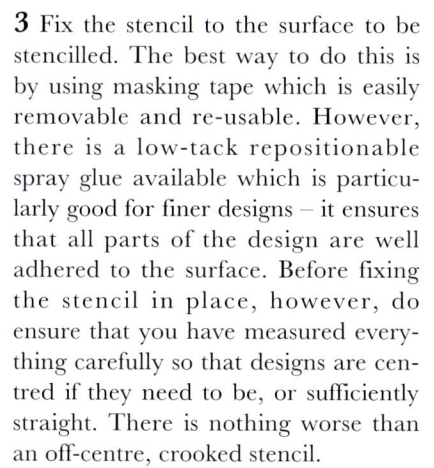

3 Fix the stencil to the surface to be stencilled. The best way to do this is by using masking tape which is easily removable and re-usable. However, there is a low-tack repositionable spray glue available which is particularly good for finer designs – it ensures that all parts of the design are well adhered to the surface. Before fixing the stencil in place, however, do ensure that you have measured everything carefully so that designs are centred if they need to be, or sufficiently straight. There is nothing worse than an off-centre, crooked stencil.

4 Acrylic paint is ideal for stencilling on walls. Place half a teaspoonful of each colour paint you will be using in saucers. Then, using a different brush for each colour, massage a small quantity of the first paint into the bristle of the brush. Test the brush on a scrap of paper in case it is overloaded, and then with small, dappling motions stipple the paint through the stencil.

To create a truly professional finish, try shading your stencils to give depth, and shade colours into each other for a subtle effect. Glorious colours can be created by mixing one shade into another; don't be afraid of experimenting, it's the only way of finding out what does and doesn't work. Try to use separate brushes for each colour. If you only have one brush, wash it thoroughly between colours. This tends to become tedious, however, and if at all possible it is best to have at least three stencil brushes.

Stencils often look lighter while they are surrounded by the oiled manilla paper or acetate, so peel back the stencil template every now and then and look at how much paint is adhering to the surface. Then replace the stencil and finish off the painting. Once you are happy with the design, slowly peel back your stencil to reveal the stippled stencil design on the wall.

FRUITS AND BERRIES

JAM JAR LABELS

Jam jar labels used in the larder make storage and identification easy. When fruits are in abundance I make jams, jellies and – even easier – gently simmer fruits with appropriate alcohols. When bottled, they are excellent for a special brunch, or after dinner with coffee. These charming stencil labels elevate a simple jar to the position of gift and they really are very easy to make. Simply cut a piece of card to shape, punch a hole at the end, stencil on the design, and then thread through some coloured cotton or raffia.

BRIGHT TEA TOWELS

Tea towels need to be in abundance in our house as, apart from drying dishes, they are used for gathering fruit or picnicking, or even for giving away as presents. I have found that they are particularly useful for this last idea, as they are so easy for young children to stencil onto and then give to relations, friends, neighbours and teachers. Fabric paint is fully washable when ironed and also non-toxic so you need have no worries about drying cutlery and china. These stencilled fruits are particularly fresh and when they are hanging up with my cross-stitched apron, make the kitchen an even brighter and more summery room.

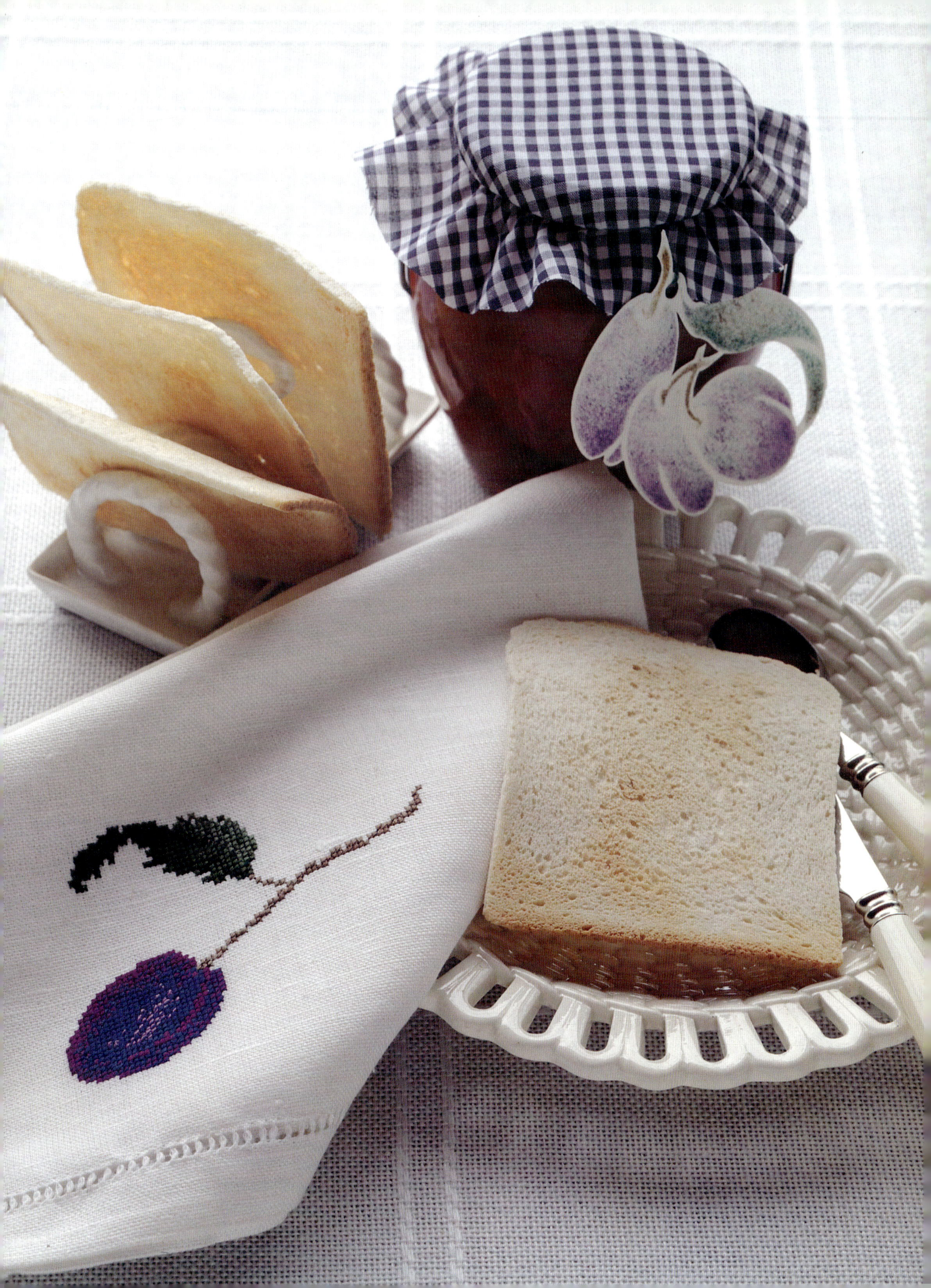

GRAPEVINE

Throughout the year, intertwining vines bearing grapes bring a constant reminder of summer into this large kitchen and family room. Both of the grapevine designs used in this kitchen are very versatile, complementing each other in delicate movement and softly dancing leaves.

The dining room leads from the kitchen and to formalize this change of atmosphere, the grapevine stencil is incorporated into a trellis surrounding the double mirrored doors. Matching cushions sit on the spare chairs that also surround the kitchen table at the far end of the room. The grapevine stencil tumbles down the trellis with accentuated movement that has been achieved by simply flipping the stencil one way and then back. Unless a stencil is asymmetrical, you will not be able to use it from the front or back in this way. Most of my stencils are asymmetrical as I find that this gives much greater scope for developing and varying a design.

The round cushions are stencilled on both sides with the trailing grapevine, joined with interlining tendrils and stems. I made up a separate little stencil especially for this repeated use taking a detail from the main design.

Larger rooms can be intimidating to stencil, so often I use the stencils in as many different ways as possible. This technique avoids repetition and also enhances the varying qualities of each part of a room as each area is used differently. One part of this room, for example, has a snug sofa and chair around a warming fire; elsewhere, there is a large kitchen table, and, of course, there are the kitchen units. While enhancing each area, the stencil design also links them together very well.

Two very different, and yet complementary, grapevine designs have been used in this large kitchen to pull its disparate elements into one, attractive whole.

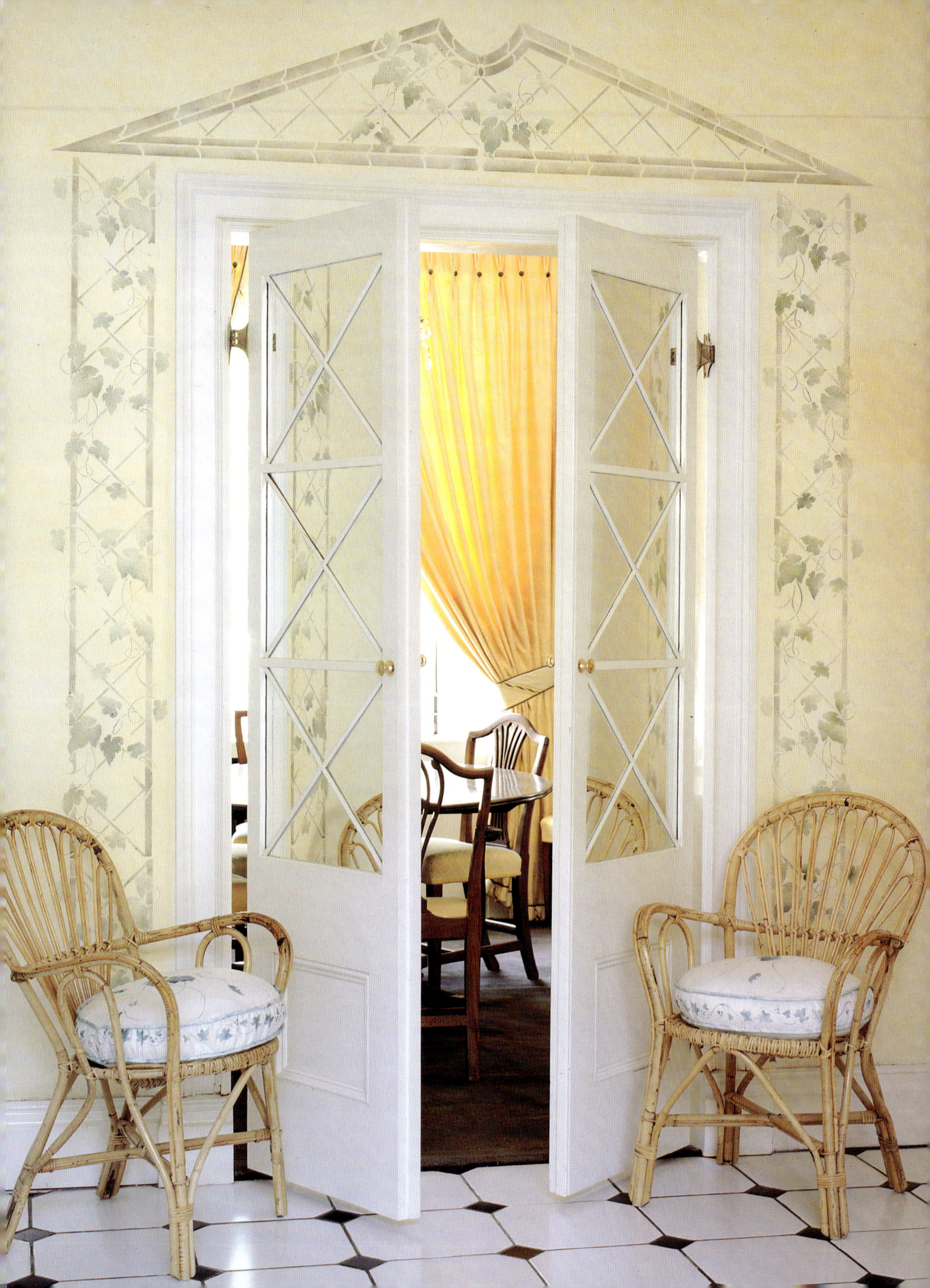

GRAPEVINE

SIZING AND ADAPTING A STENCIL AND USING OILED MANILLA PAPER

YOU WILL NEED	
Grapevine pull-out stencil (see page 35)	Oiled manila paper (optional)
Cutting mat	Soft pencil (optional)
Masking tape	Repositionable spray glue (optional)
Craft knife or embroidery scissors	Acrylic paints
Photocopier (optional)	Stencil brushes
Tracing paper (optional)	Varnish

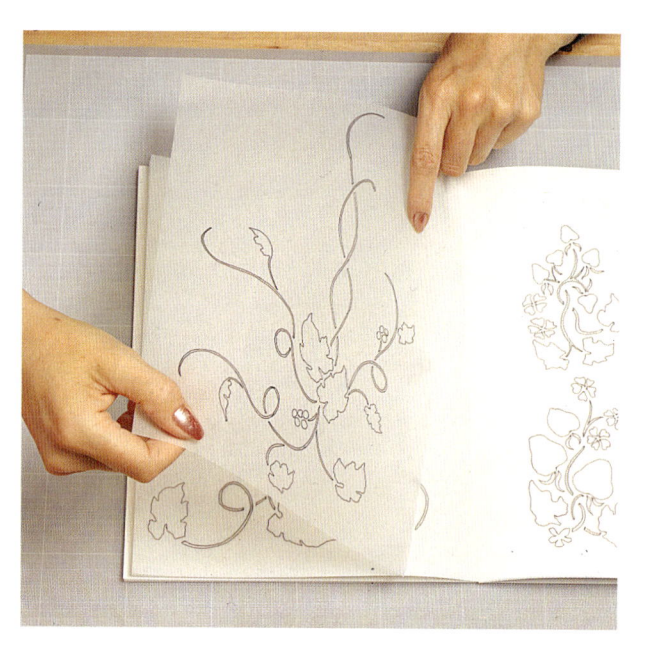

1 Pull or cut out the stencil featured on page 35 of this book and cut out the leaves, tendrils, grapes and stems using the cutting mat, masking tape and craft knife (see step 2 on page 14 for more guidance). In case the knife should slip, always cut away from your hand holding the paper. Embroidery scissors cut just as well, but it may take a little longer to cut out the stencil.

2 If you wish to enlarge the size of the grapevine stencil that is in this book, use the enlarging facility on a photocopier. If the enlargement is very great, you might need to enlarge the stencil in sections and then stick the pieces together prior to stencilling.

20

GRAPEVINE

3 Transfer the enlarged design onto tracing paper and then onto oiled manila paper and cut out. To transfer the outline, draw over the outline on the back of the tracing paper with a very soft pencil, position the tracing paper on the oiled manila paper and go over the top of the outline one more time. Cut out the stencil as for step 1.

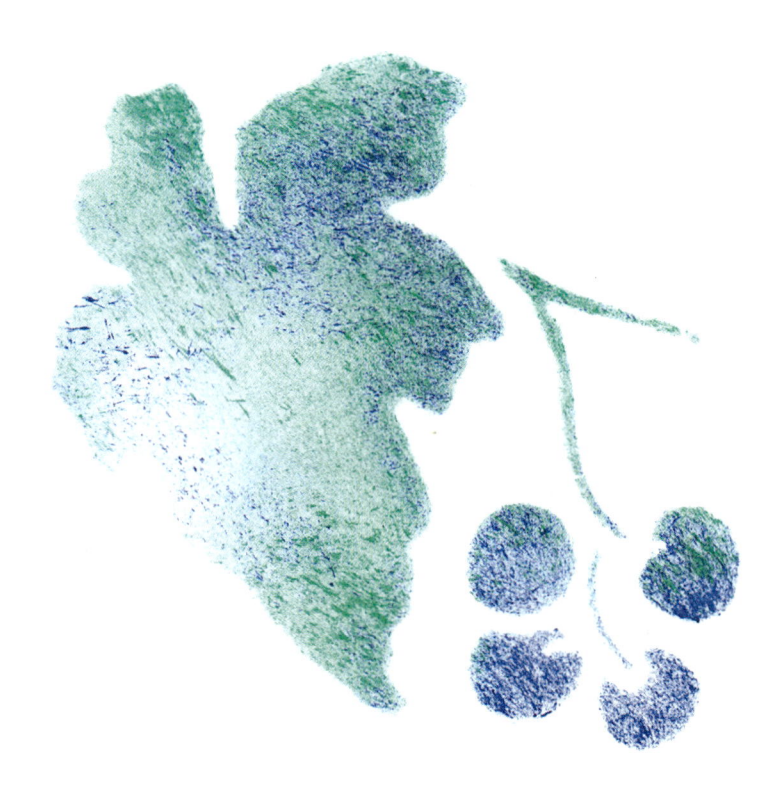

4 Fix the stencil to the surface onto which you are going to paint using the masking tape or repositionable spray glue and then stencil as described on page 15.

It is important to seal the stencils on kitchen cupboards. To do this, either replace the stencil and stencil on some varnish, or paint the whole panel. Acrylic varnish rarely yellows the paint, whereas oil-based varnish nearly always does. Do get good advice on the product that you wish to use and, if in any doubt, test the inside of a cupboard door beforehand.

The kitchen cupboard panels in this kitchen were made in various widths. So when I found that the design was too big and the tendrils were overrunning the edges of the panels, I covered the excess stencil with masking tape. If I hadn't done this it would have been all too easy to make a mistake while stencilling the panel.

GRAPEVINE

THE KITCHEN CUPBOARD PANELS

Each panel that I was going to stencil in this kitchen was a different width, and the lower panels above the dishwasher were slightly deeper, too. So to make the most of the stencil, I enlarged it to the size of the largest cupboard and then covered those parts of the stencil that trailed off the edge of the panels.

As you can see from the stencil, I have designed the trailing tendrils so that they can be used in a particularly flexible way by using less or more of them as necessary. For shorter panels, I missed out the middle section of the tendril, moving up the stencil at the appropriate point so that just the trailing ends appear. To do this, first stencil the main leaves and as many side tendrils as are required, then lift off the stencil and reposition it a little further up the panel so that you can use the nice looping ends as a detail. As you become more confident with stencilling, you will know how to use a little trick like this. Stencils really do make a most versatile form of decoration.

GRAPEVINE

VARYING THE THEME

A single stencil can be used in many ways, particularly one such as this where there are many different elements, so parts of a design can be used in various ways. With the judicious use of masking tape you can cover over parts of a stencil that you don't wish to use and just by turning a stencil through 90° it looks quite different.

 The other end of this particular family room is quite informal and so I extended the trailing parts of the stencil over an arch on each side of a centrally positioned clock. In each corner, the stencils have also been very lightly applied over the soft yellow colourwashed walls. Putting stencils in corners is a favourite of mine, I feel it extends the eye and adds interest, particularly when so delicate.

GRAPEVINE

A pull-out stencil for this design is given on page 35. In addition, here is a variation of the Grapevine to be used in whatever way you choose. Cut out elements or the whole design; use it separately, or add to the pull-out stencil.

GRAPEVINE

TRAILING ACANTHUS LEAVES

This beautiful Victorian-style acanthus leaf curling over a rod has always been a great favourite of mine. I love the way it twists and turns and with some careful shading its three-dimensional effect can be brought out most successfully.

The acanthus leaf was much used by the Greeks in their classical architecture, mainly on the capital of the Corinthian columns. I think it is this timeless quality that really appeals to me and possibly because of its links with classical architecture and I find that it works particularly well along straight edges. I have designed this stencil specifically with corners in mind (see overleaf), creating a neat mitre with the end of a leaf. So why not use it to decorate the kitchen table, napkins and cushions, or trail it around a small feature window or set of shelves? By flipping over the stencil, you will also make a neat, symmetrical mirror-image, which is just what I did with it on this table and on the napkins on pages 30-31.

Alternatively, to introduce yet more colour to a table, I made some boldly coloured place mats that generate warmth and appeal (see pages 30-1). I then stencilled the acanthus design onto some napkins to coordinate the whole setting. By selecting the brightest colours, the place mats are echoed and harmony is achieved. Large muslin napkins are ideal to tuck under one's chin or for sticky fingers, and squeezed into the contrasting napkin rings they make an unusual welcome to the table.

Enhance subtleties in the napkins by stencilling with two colours, building them up in layers. The leaves were stencilled in a light blue, with touches from a darker blue brush to colour the rod. Stencilling in this way gives a softer finish and also gives you greater control over the finished project.

On a hot summer day, what could be better than bringing your kitchen out into the garden and dining al fresco?

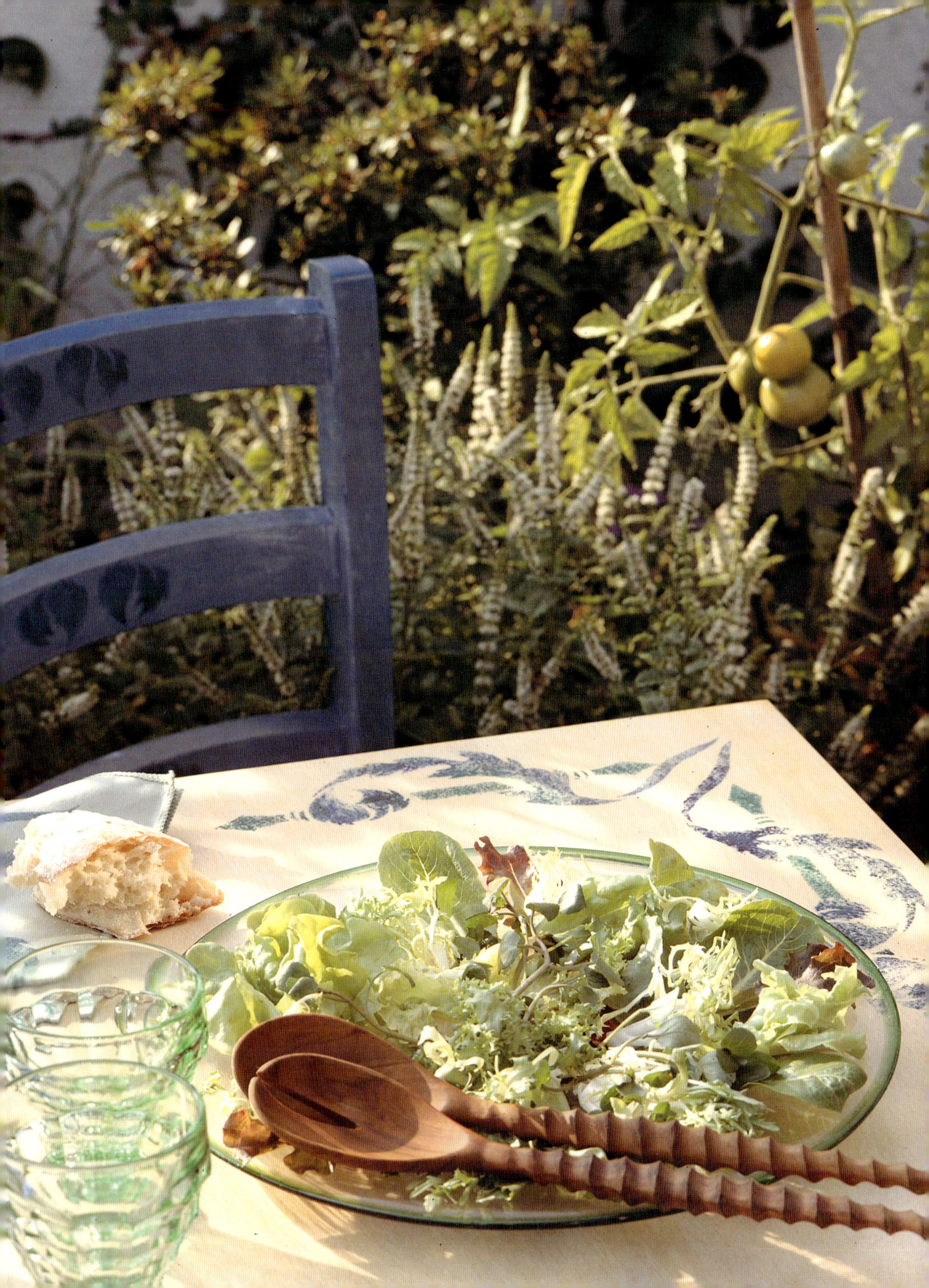

TRAILING ACANTHUS LEAVES

TURNING CORNERS AND USING SPRAY PAINTS

If you feel that you would prefer to use, say, just the acanthus leaves of this design some time it might be worth preparing your own stencil in addition to using the pull-out one provided in this book. To do this, first transfer just the leaves onto oiled manilla paper as explained in step 3 on page 21, and then transfer the rod so that it lies slightly above the leaves.

Also, if you are going to be using the stencil for turning around corners, it would be worth tracing on the corner turn now so that you can cut it out all as one stencil. To create a suitable corner with this design, turn the end acanthus leaf through 90° and flip it over so that the top of the tracing paper becomes the bottom side. Cut out the design and then you are ready to stencil.

YOU WILL NEED

Trailing acanthus leaves pull-out stencil (see page 37)

Tracing paper (optional)

Soft pencil (optional)

Oiled manilla paper (optional)

Cutting mat

Masking tape

Craft knife or small embroidery scissors

Repositionable spray glue

Newspaper

Protective mask

Spray paints

Scrap paper

1 Once you have prepared your stencil as described above, accurately place it against the wall. I use a repositionable spray glue on the back of the stencil which closely bonds the template to the wall. Spray paint is a very forceful medium for stencilling and it can all too easily seep behind the stencil template. Cover the rod element of the stencil with masking tape to prevent paint from accidentally showing through here.

2 Firmly apply sheets of newspaper around the stencil template with masking tape. Neither the masking tape, nor the repositionable spray glue should affect your wall surface, but it is advisable to test a small and unobtrusive area beforehand. Please always use a protective mask when using spray paint. Also, work in a well-ventilated area and do not sleep in the same room or introduce babies or asthmatics for at least 48 hours, as the paint might trouble them.

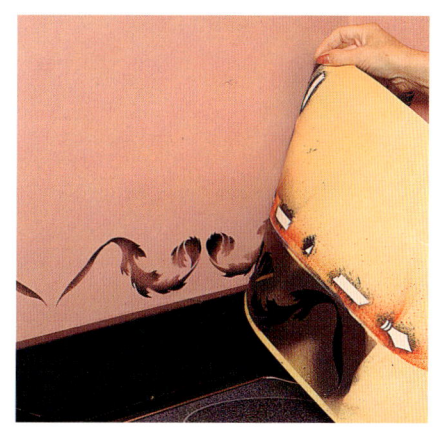

TRAILING ACANTHUS LEAVES

The acanthus leaves have been successfully stencilled above the cooker making the most of the corner of this kitchen. Not only has the leaf been reversed to go up the wall, but the whole stencil has also been flipped over so that an exact mirror image has been created on the right-hand wall.

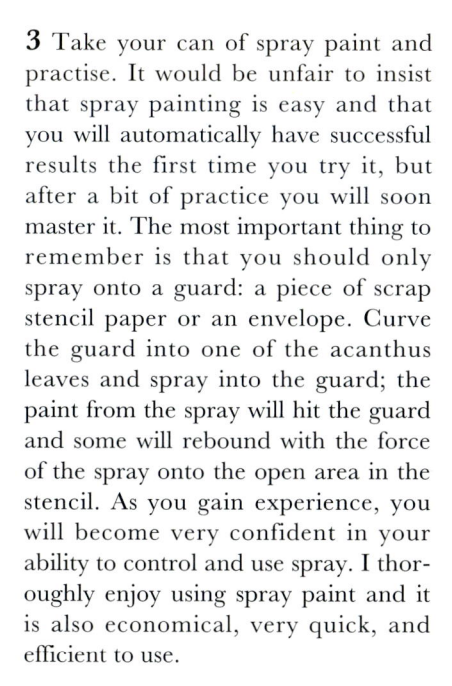

3 Take your can of spray paint and practise. It would be unfair to insist that spray painting is easy and that you will automatically have successful results the first time you try it, but after a bit of practice you will soon master it. The most important thing to remember is that you should only spray onto a guard: a piece of scrap stencil paper or an envelope. Curve the guard into one of the acanthus leaves and spray into the guard; the paint from the spray will hit the guard and some will rebound with the force of the spray onto the open area in the stencil. As you gain experience, you will become very confident in your ability to control and use spray. I thoroughly enjoy using spray paint and it is also economical, very quick, and efficient to use.

4 Remove the newspaper and masking tape, then gently peel back the stencil template from the wall to reveal a crisp, clear image with no smudges, smears or drips of paint. Repeat the stencil around the frieze as required. Again only remove your mask when you leave the stencilled room as particles of paint remain airborne for a while.

Overleaf: *Add a touch of colour to fresh white cotton napkins by stencilling your kitchen table or wall design onto them using bright fabric paints.*

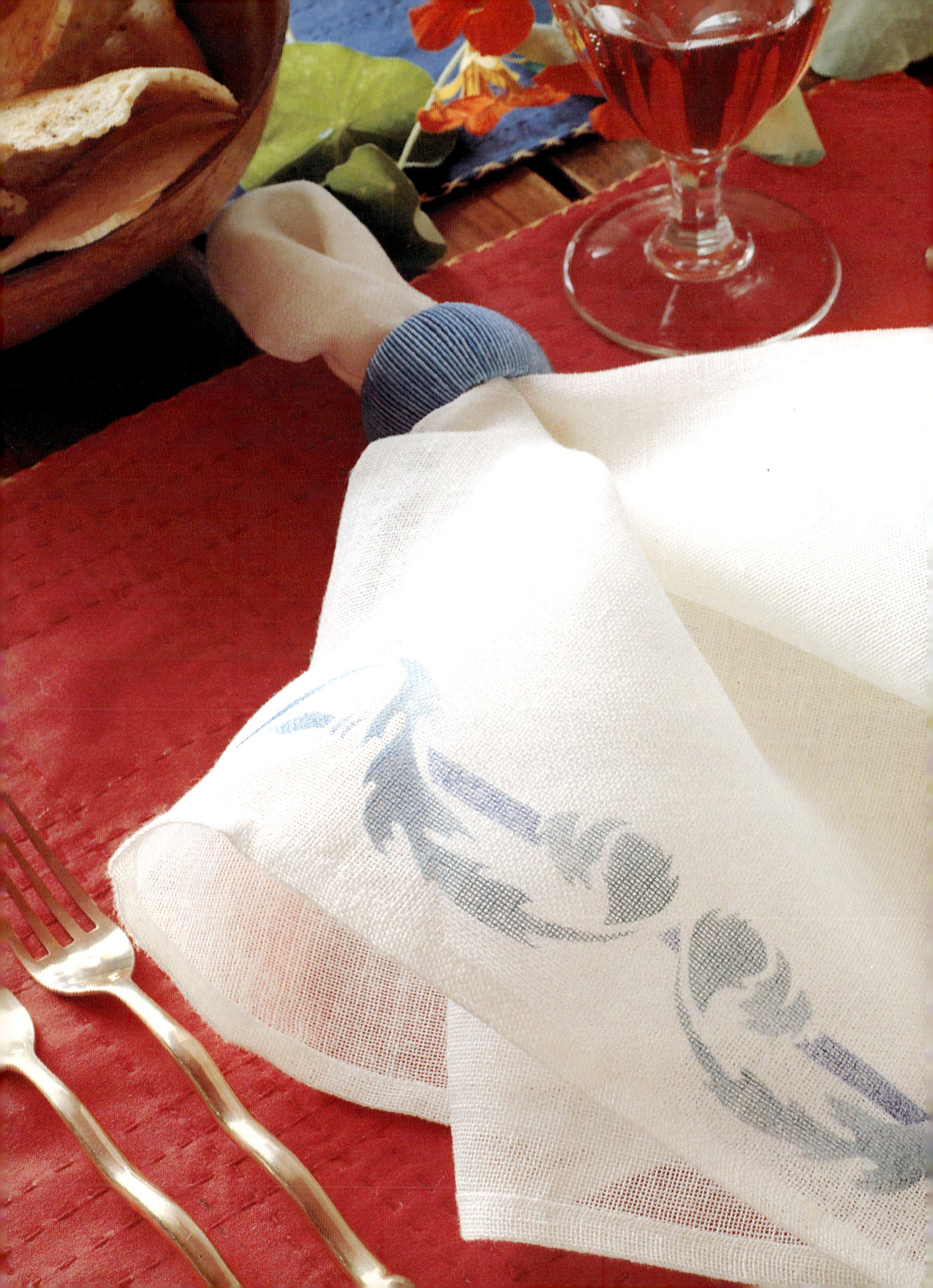

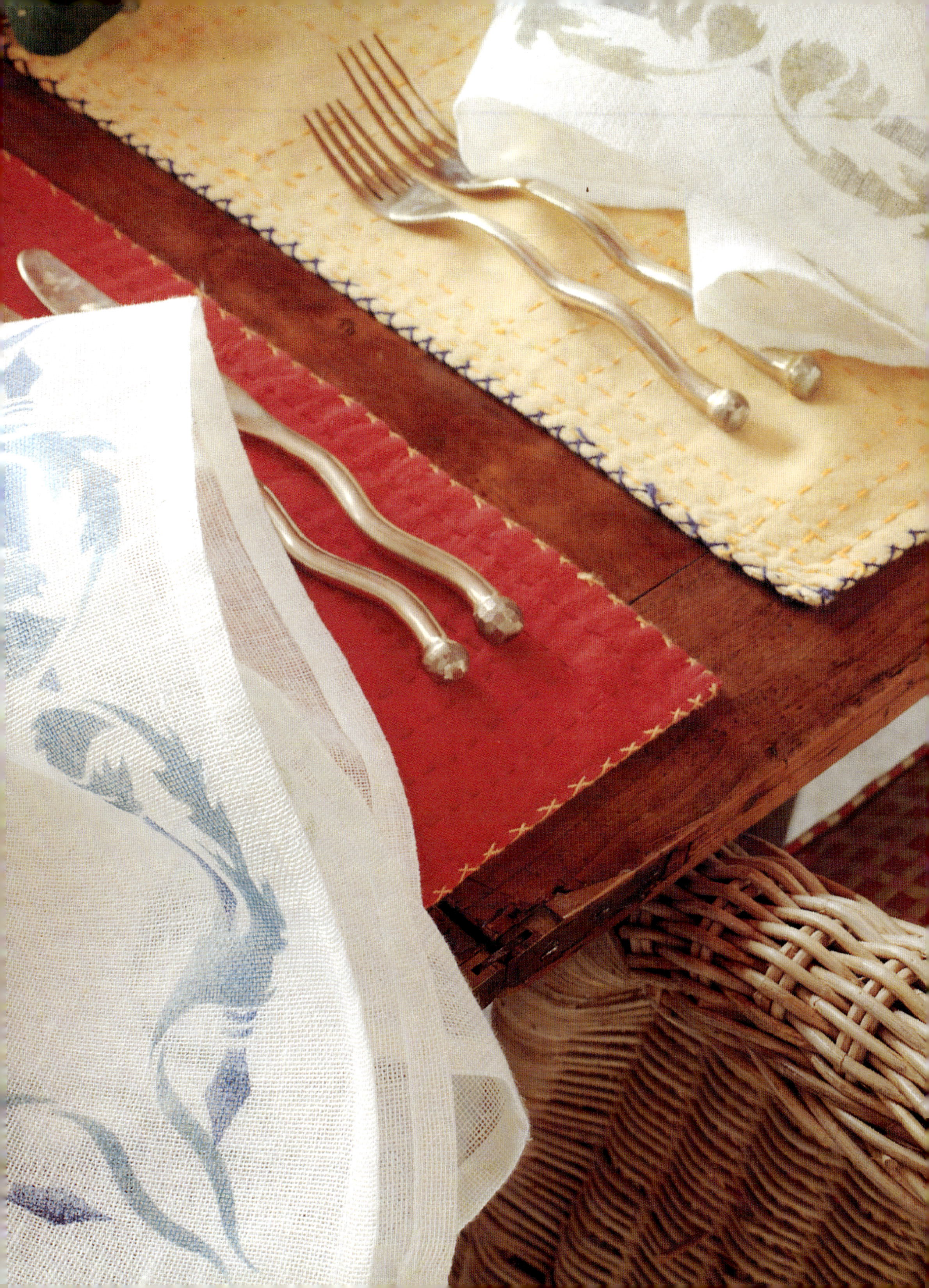

TRAILING ACANTHUS LEAVES

CONTINUING THE THEME

When stencilling, don't ever feel that you must continually use the complete stencil whenever you apply it. In fact, it is much better to use only parts of it when stencilling accessories to the main design – it is far most subtle and hence more appealing.

When I had finished stencilling the table featured on page 27, I decided it would be fun to stencil some accompanying kitchen chairs and their cushions. The mitred corners of the design make it so easy to use that the cushions were really easy to decorate.

As you can see from the picture, I chose to simply use the acanthus part of the stencil on the cushions, and just one leaf of that too. I worked around the corners, using a colour that subtly contrasted with the cushion to create a delightfully muted effect.

The chair back is stencilled with yet another element of the design – the two smallest leaves. These were the perfect size to position in the middle of each cross bar and I think they are just right. I had initially considered adding a rod and finial on each side of the leaves, but once I had stencilled them I realized that the rods would make the chair backs too over-stated.

When stencilling other items to accompany the main piece, use elements of the stencil only – a leaf here a mitred corner there.

32

FRUITS AND BERRIES
(SEE PAGES 12-17)

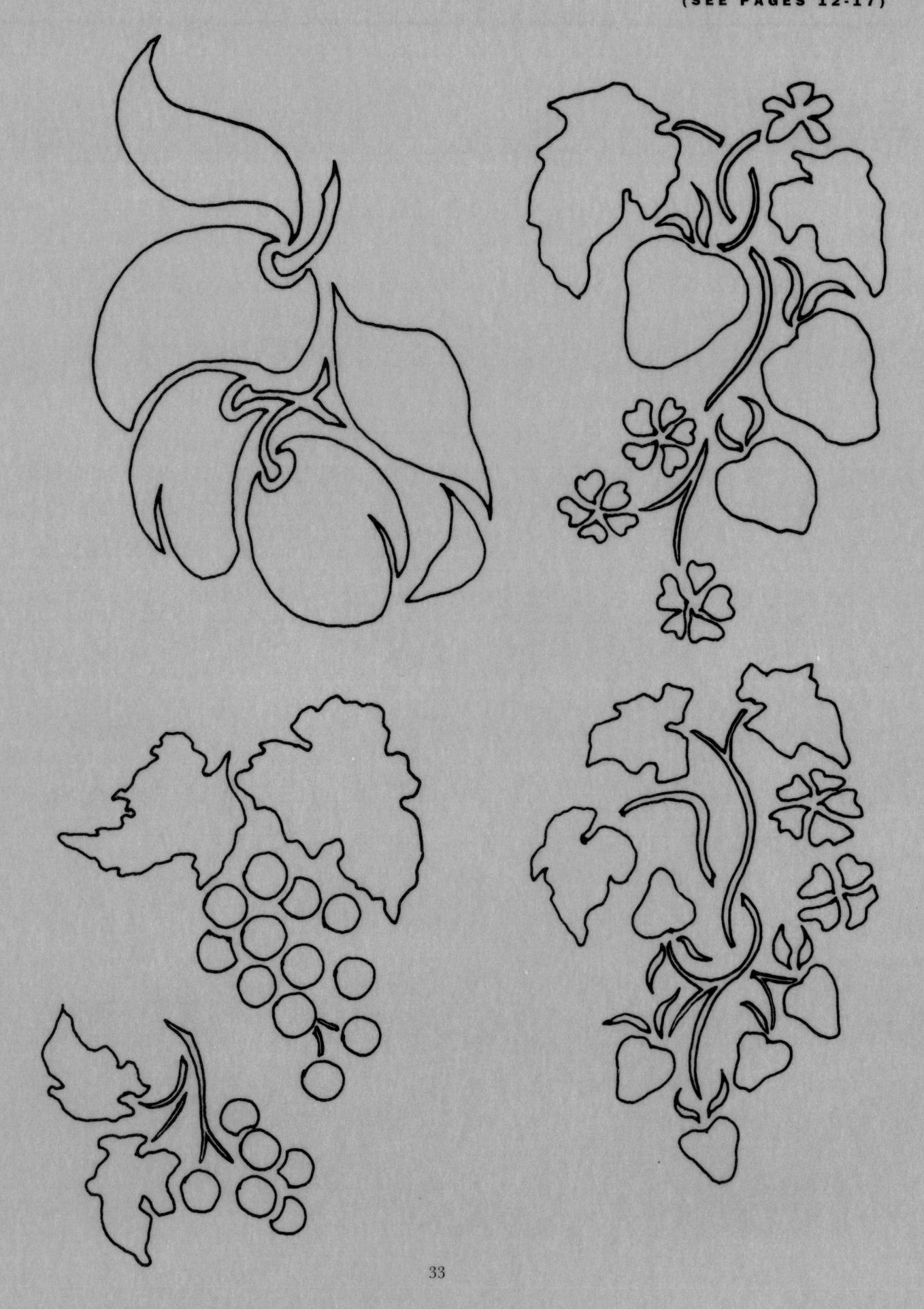

FRUITS AND BERRIES
(SEE PAGES 12-17)

GRAPEVINE
(SEE PAGES 18-23)

GRAPEVINE
(SEE PAGES 18-23)

TRAILING ACANTHUS LEAVES
(SEE PAGES 26-32)

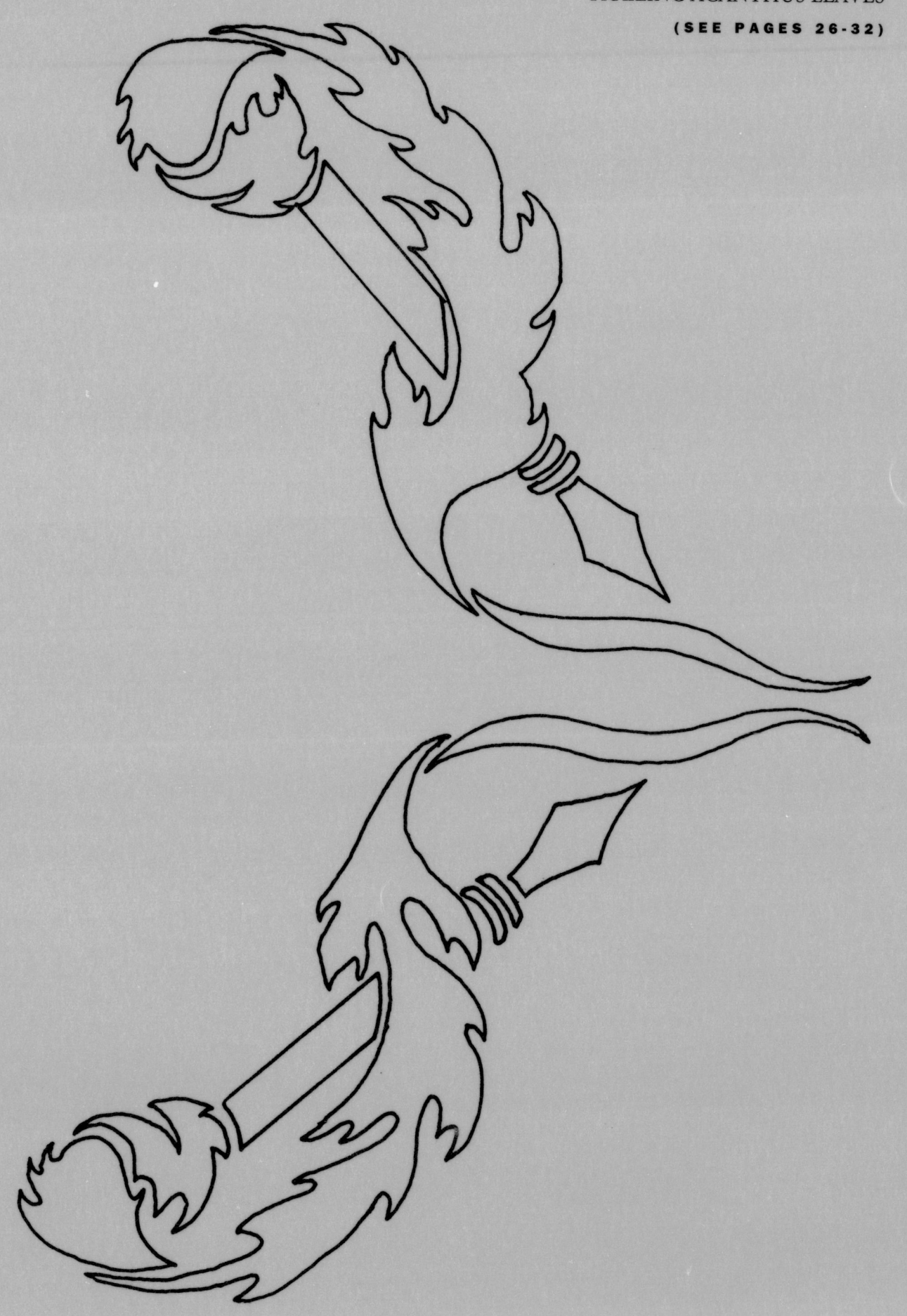

TRAILING ACANTHUS LEAVES
(SEE PAGES 26-32)

VEGETABLES AND HERBS

(SEE PAGES 49-53)

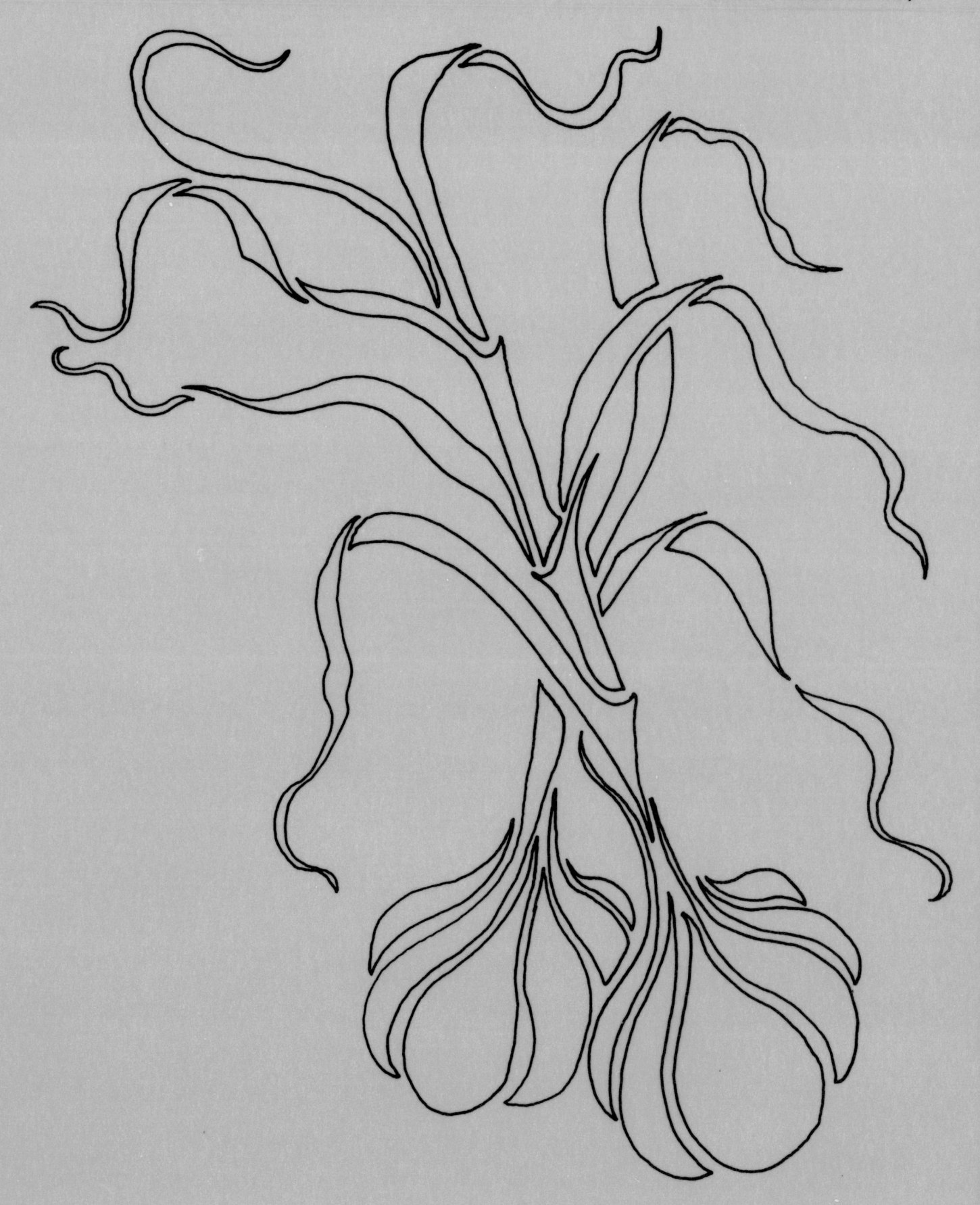

VEGETABLES AND HERBS

(SEE PAGES 49-53)

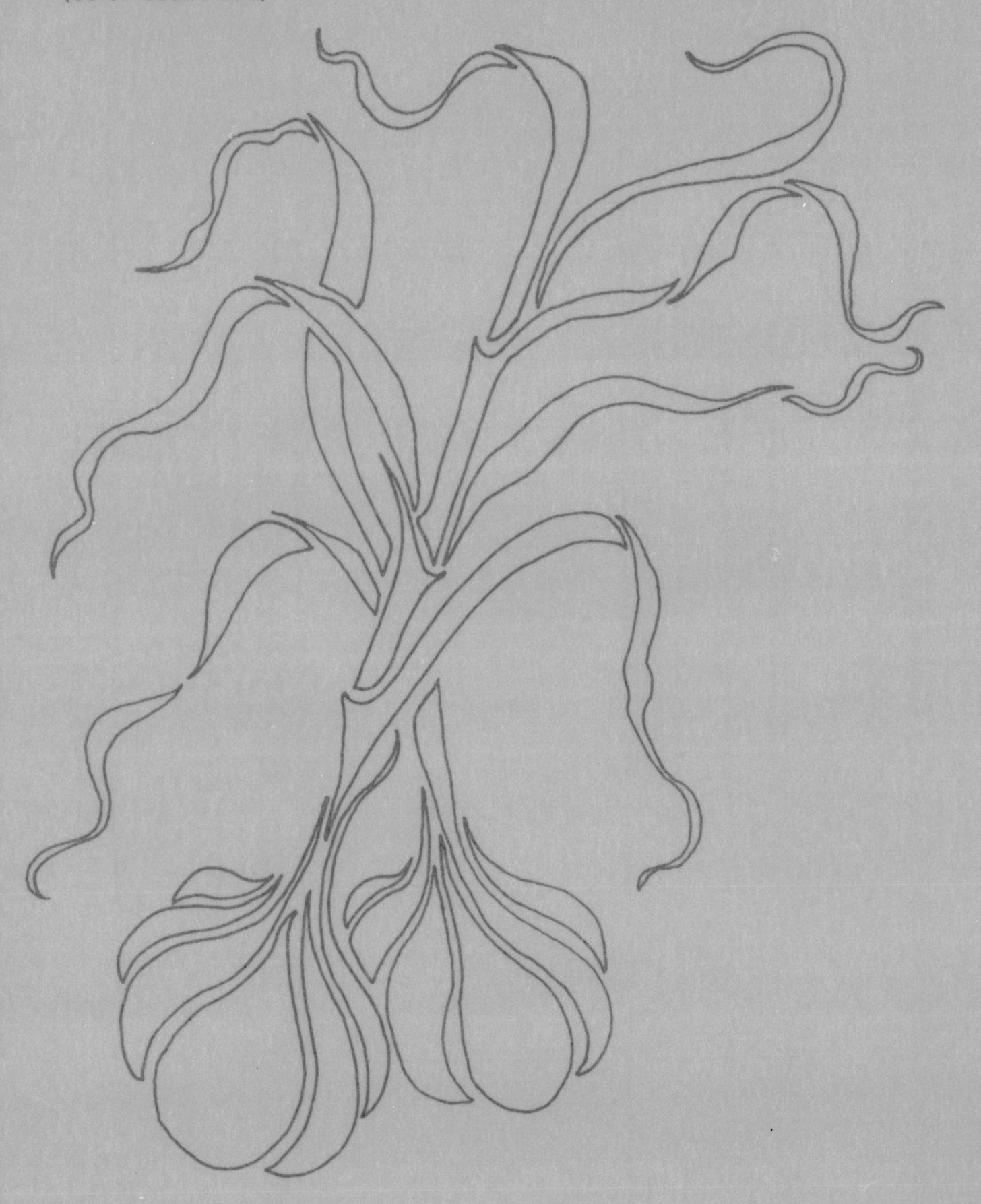

VEGETABLES AND HERBS
(SEE PAGES 49-53)

VEGETABLES AND HERBS
(SEE PAGES 49-53)

DELFTWARE TILES
(SEE PAGES 68-73)

DELFTWARE TILES
(SEE PAGES 68-73)

PROVENÇAL SUNFLOWERS

(SEE PAGES 74-79)

PROVENÇAL SUNFLOWERS
(SEE PAGES 74-79)

VEGETABLES AND HERBS

If the weather is fine I shall find any excuse to be outside, whether for a meal, weeding or watering my plant pots, or just to sit and work, installed on a small terrace perched among London's roofs.

Among my many occupations, my favourites are preparing vegetables and herbs for the cooler days ahead. I love to dry off onions and garlic and then plait them into tresses to dry for the autumn; toss the chaff out of my home-grown herbs ready for the winter's stews, and thread dried chilies into wreaths and bundles to use as decorations and to make the odd, very spicy addition to a meal. Then at the end of some perfect afternoons I can relax with a glass of wine at a table freshly covered with stencilled cloth and napkins.

Here individual chilies run down one cloth, a cluster of chilies are on a woven cloth, and a pair of garlic bulbs rest on a linen cloth.

VEGETABLES AND HERBS

TABLECLOTH AND NAPKINS

Stencilled sprigs of bay leaves spring out from the corner of this tablecloth, and they have been tied together by a contrasting narrow blue ribbon. The leaves are reversed back and forth around the border of the cloth making a gently undulating, curving frieze from an otherwise simple sprig of leaves.

The same motif is again used on the napkins, stencilling a crossed pair of twigs to make an interesting corner. In addition, bright chilies adorn one napkin, and rounded cloves of garlic another, making this a perfect table setting for an evening aperitif.

All the fabrics are fully washable. Just by ironing the reverse side of the stencilled fabric to the heat that your fabric tolerates for one minute will fix fabric paints forever. Try stencilling cushions, cotton rugs for the floor or drying-up towels with these glorious vegetables.

YOU WILL NEED

Vegetable and herb pull-out stencils (see pages 39 and 41)

Cutting mat

Masking tape

Craft knife or small embroidery scissors

Repositionable spray glue (optional)

Fabric paints

Stencil brushes

SEE ALSO

Sizing a stencil (page 20)

Adapting a stencil (page 21)

Using spray paint (page 29)

1 Before you start stencilling, gather together all your equipment so that you know you have everything to hand. If you are going to stencil these designs onto other surfaces, check that you have the right kind of paints (see the chart on page 11).
2 Pull or cut out the stencils from the centre of this book and then cut them out, fixing the stencil paper to the cutting board or mat using strips of masking tape. Draw the blade gently towards you ensuring your supporting hand is away from the blade. For further information on cutting out stencils see step 2 on page 14.
3 Fix the stencil to the fabric to be stencilled using masking tape or low-tack repositionable spray glue (see step 3 on page 15). Make sure it is straight and, if important, centred.
4 Apply the paint – see step 4 on page 15 for more help with the stippling technique. To create a truly professional finish, try shading your stencils to give depth, and shade colours into each other for a subtle effect.

Right *and* Opposite: *Simple motifs and straightforward stippling result in charming stencils that are best left understated.*

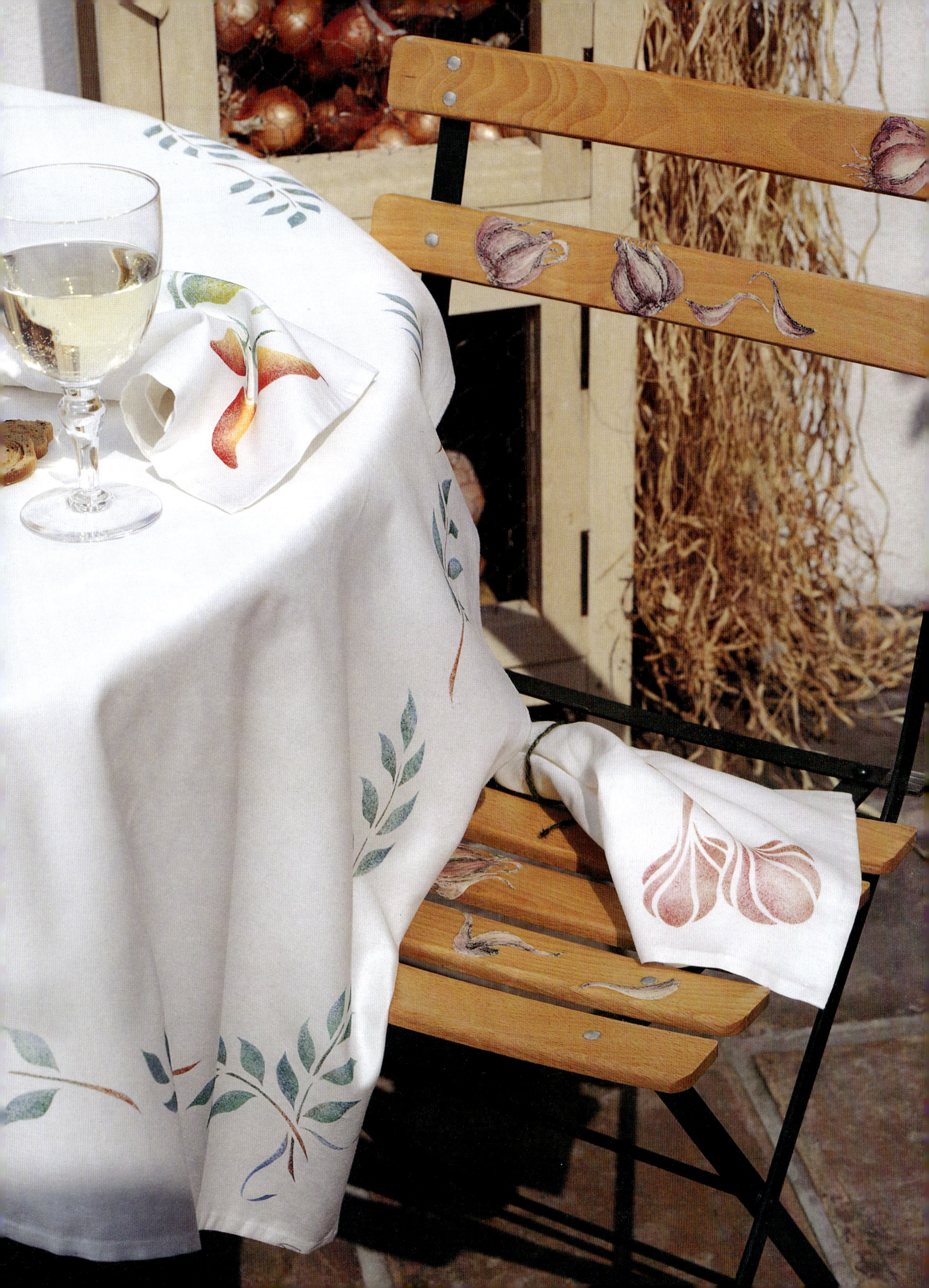

VEGETABLES AND HERBS

KITCHEN CABINET FULL OF VEGETABLES

In the past, this chicken wire cabinet was filled with garden pots, but at long last I have finally managed to use it for its correct purpose of drying vegetables. So here they are, hanging in abundance to dry in the sun with the background stencils matching the vegetables.

Stencilling the insides of cupboards is rather fun and gives a complete finish to your kitchen. Acrylics are the most adaptable paints to use on prepared wood, but if you have a modern melamine finish, try using spray paints which will adhere much, much better.

The chilies were stencilled uniformly in three rows across the back of the cupboard adding a backdrop for my dangling chilies, while the whole of the garlic stencil was used, tucking one stencil beneath another to create a larger bunch (see the previous page).

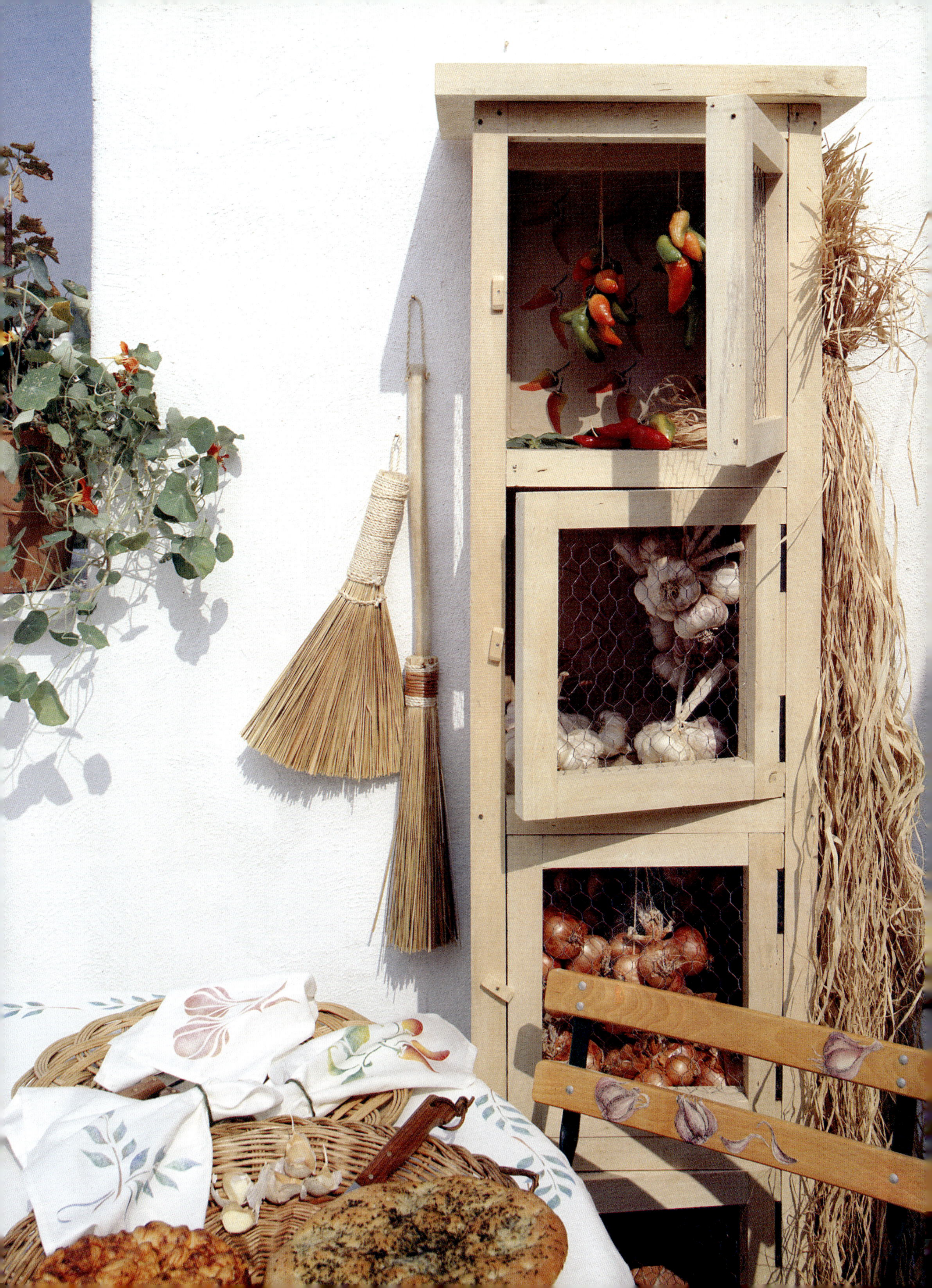

BLUE FLOWERS

This charming old blue flower design crockery set was given to me recently. Unfortunately, my kitchen at that time was rather stark so I set out to create a stencil design that would tone in with the crockery, softening the kitchen at the same time.

Any fabric or other design in your kitchen can easily be transformed into a stencil. If you are not very artistic just take your plate or piece of curtain material along to the nearest photocopier. Photocopiers enlarge or reduce and it is worth having several possibilities printed. Then temporarily place the photocopies onto the wall so that you can judge how large or small you would like your design to be, and how many repeats may be needed around a wall. Take my advice and always take the easy option – you will find that it will give you greater choice with less work.

In my kitchen, I chose to run the stencil around the room, continuing it across the half rolled-up blinds (see overleaf). The end result was a kitchen that looked larger than in its former existence.

Don't worry about using the same paint on different types of surface. Often it is easier to cheat and use the same paint each time. Here, for example, I used fabric paint on both the blinds and the walls to avoid having to risk a fabric paint and an acrylic paint drying to slightly different tones. I used fabric paint for both surfaces, rather than using acrylics, judging that as the blinds were lowered they would need occasional wiping. Then, to protect the wall and stencil on it I gave it several coats of acrylic varnish which neither discolours the paint nor alters the stencil. To stencil the blinds I removed them from the window and stencilled on a flat table top. Please never be tempted to stencil a blind in situ; to fall through a window for the sake of a stencilled blind is not advisable. The blinds normally remain up, but for added interest and variation, I stencilled small individual flowers beneath the main stencil.

Opposite: For a spot of fabric coordination, consider stencilling the same design onto tea towels. By fixing fabric paints on the back of the tea towel with an iron you will be able to wash the tea towel just as frequently as ever.

Overleaf: By leaving white blinds slightly unrolled, the ideal surface is left to stencil on. In this way, a frieze can be continued right around the kitchen.

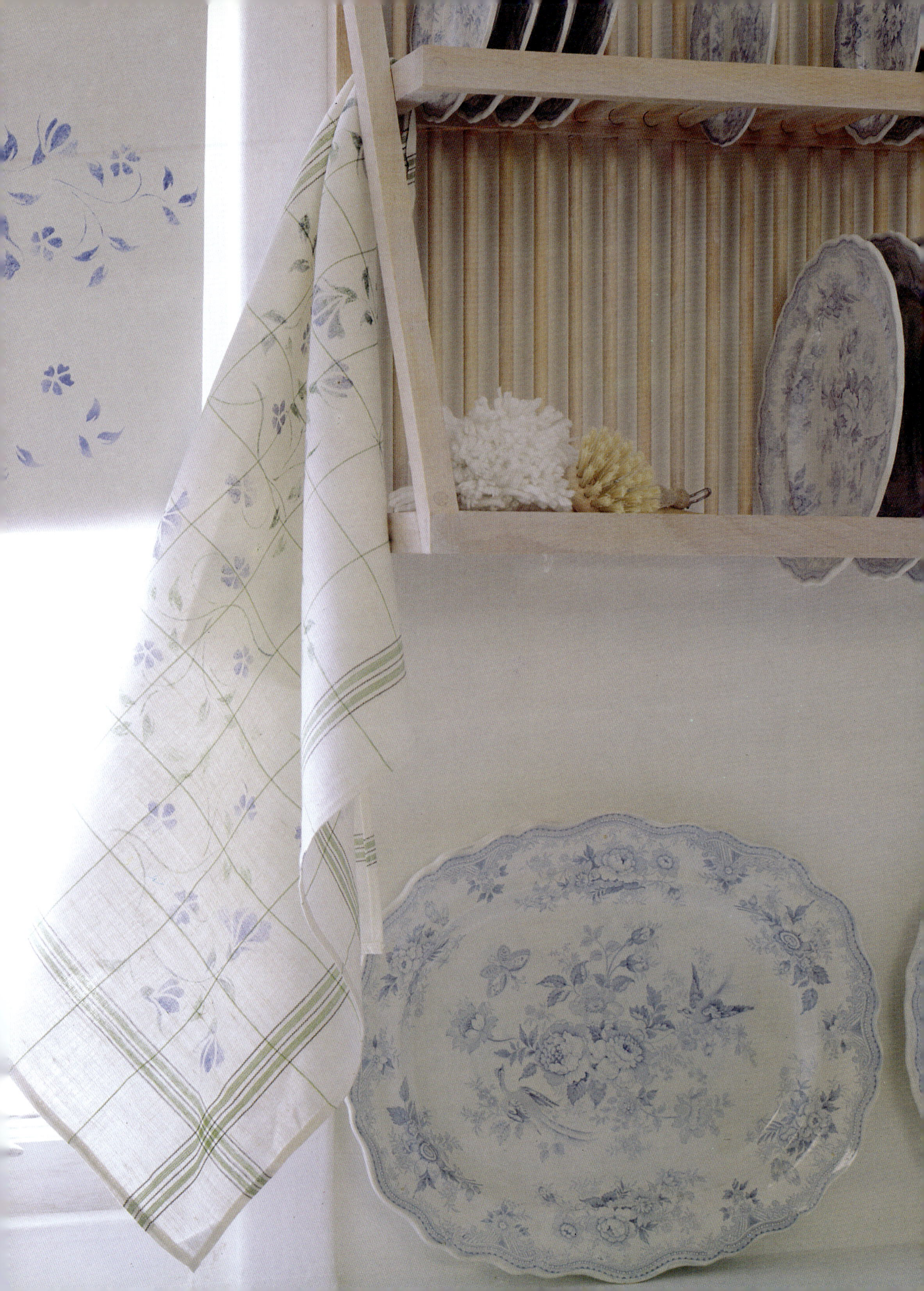

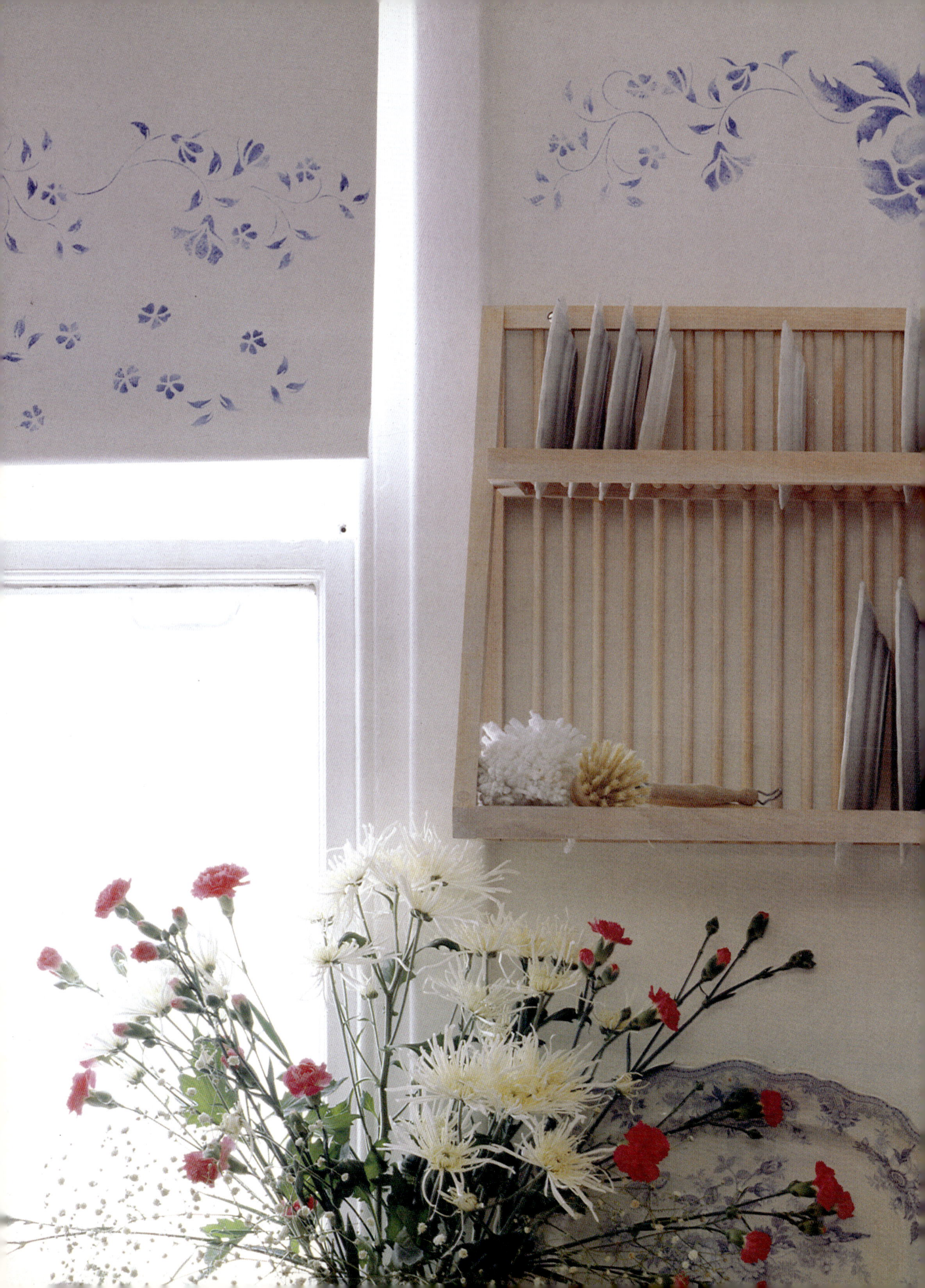

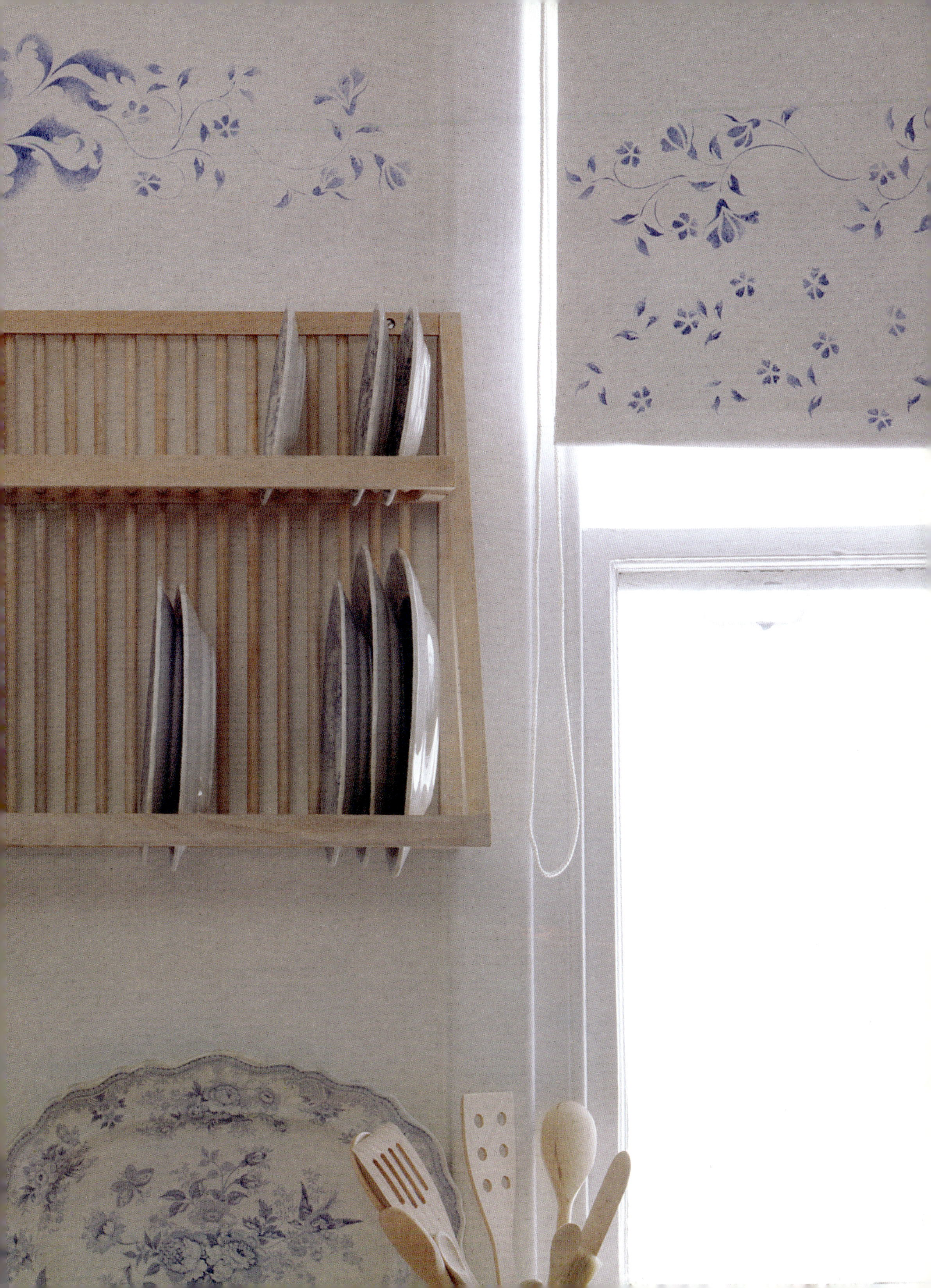

BLUE FLOWERS

COORDINATING YOUR KITCHEN

My kitchen has a large table where I can spread out my larger projects, join the children and their numerous friends, or push a messy project to one side and camp for an informal meal at the other end of the extended table.

To coordinate your kitchen, why not stencil fabric and napkins, oven cloths and tea towels which are often drying within the kitchen? It is so easy to customize your own tablecloth; a little hemming around almost any fabric is all that is required. My tablecloth is light textured cotton found in a remnants bin at my local fabric shop and I think that it add a certain elegance to even the simplest meal. It certainly adds to the pleasure of eating from these really beautiful blue and white floral plates.

If you are stencilling onto fabric, especially if you only have a small amount to play with, test your colour effects on a piece of scrap paper. It is always helpful to have a practice run, and by cutting out the stencil as near to the paint as possible you can see what the finished effect will be like by holding it against the fabric. My daughters often use paper napkins for their test runs, as the napkins are more absorbent and resemble fabric in their texture. They also have the additional advantage that you can use up your test runs for a fully coordinated table setting within your kitchen.

Subtle blending of colours in your stencil can vary the design and enhance its surroundings.

BLUE FLOWERS

1 Before you start stencilling, gather together all your equipment so that you know you have everything to hand. Check that you have the right kind of paints for the surface you intend stencilling on to (see the chart on page 11). To avoid different tones of blue when stencilling on the walls and the blind I chose to use fabric paints on the walls, too (see page 54).

2 Pull or cut out the stencil from the centre of this book and then cut it out, fixing the stencil paper to the cutting board or mat using strips of masking tape. Draw the blade of the craft knife gently towards you ensuring your supporting hand is away from the blade. For further information on cutting out stencils see step 2 on page 14.

3 Fix the stencil to the surface to be stencilled using masking tape or low-tack repositionable spray glue (see step 3 on page 15). Make sure it is straight and, if important, centred.

4 Apply the paint – see step 4 on page 15 for more help with the stippling technique. To create a truly professional finish, try shading your stencils to give depth, and shade colours into each other for a subtle effect. To prevent the stencil from becoming tediously repetitive, I included a little green within the leaves when using it on the tablecloth. In this way, the design was varied just sufficiently, detracting from the predominant blue and white on the walls. I also added a hint of purple on leaves and petals to sympathize with the older plates.

YOU WILL NEED

Blue flowers pull-out stencil (see page 43)

Cutting mat

Masking tape

Craft knife or small embroidery scissors

Repositionable spray glue (optional)

Fabric paints

Stencil brushes

SEE ALSO

Using acrylic paints (page 15)

Adapting a stencil (page 21)

Using spray paints (page 29)

59

KITCHEN CUTLERY

One day, the children had unloaded the dishwasher and scattered the cutlery over the narrow worksurface, and as we went to sort out the knives from the forks I thought, what an interesting pattern the cutlery made tumbling back and forth over one another. So tracing around some of the cutlery as you might around your hand, I made knives, forks and spoons into stencils.

I thought that I might introduce some order into the cutlery drawer and stencilled the corresponding cutlery motif to the cutlery tray. I also stencilled the tea towels so that they look much brighter and more cheerful, just in case additional help might be at hand.

As the wall surface in this kitchen is not protected by tiles (see overleaf) it has been painted with oil-based, washable paint and the stencil applied with spray paint (see page 29). By stencilling onto a washable surface using spray paints you are creating a design that is extremely durable and fully waterproof.

I like using spray paint as the end result can be so varied. I found that the cutlery stencil looked too heavy in acrylic paints on the wall, and much prefer the slightly misty and yet defined image of the cutlery that can be achieved with the delicate application of spray paint. It does take some practice, so I suggest that you have at least ten test runs on newspaper before you tackle your kitchen wall.

The cutlery has been stencilled in a very free way in the pictures opposite and overleaf. It is easy to do in this way by using masking tape to cover those areas of the stencil that you don't want to paint through. However, the stencils are laid out in a very regimented way on pages 66-67 and you might like to use them in this way, too, as a more formal pattern than the ones created here.

Opposite: Don't forget to stencil those parts of the kitchen that aren't usually seen – here a cutlery container has an originally stencilled base on plastic coated paper so that you can see exactly which pieces of cutlery go where.

Overleaf: The pieces of cutlery have been stencilled here to look like they have casually been scattered across a worksurface.

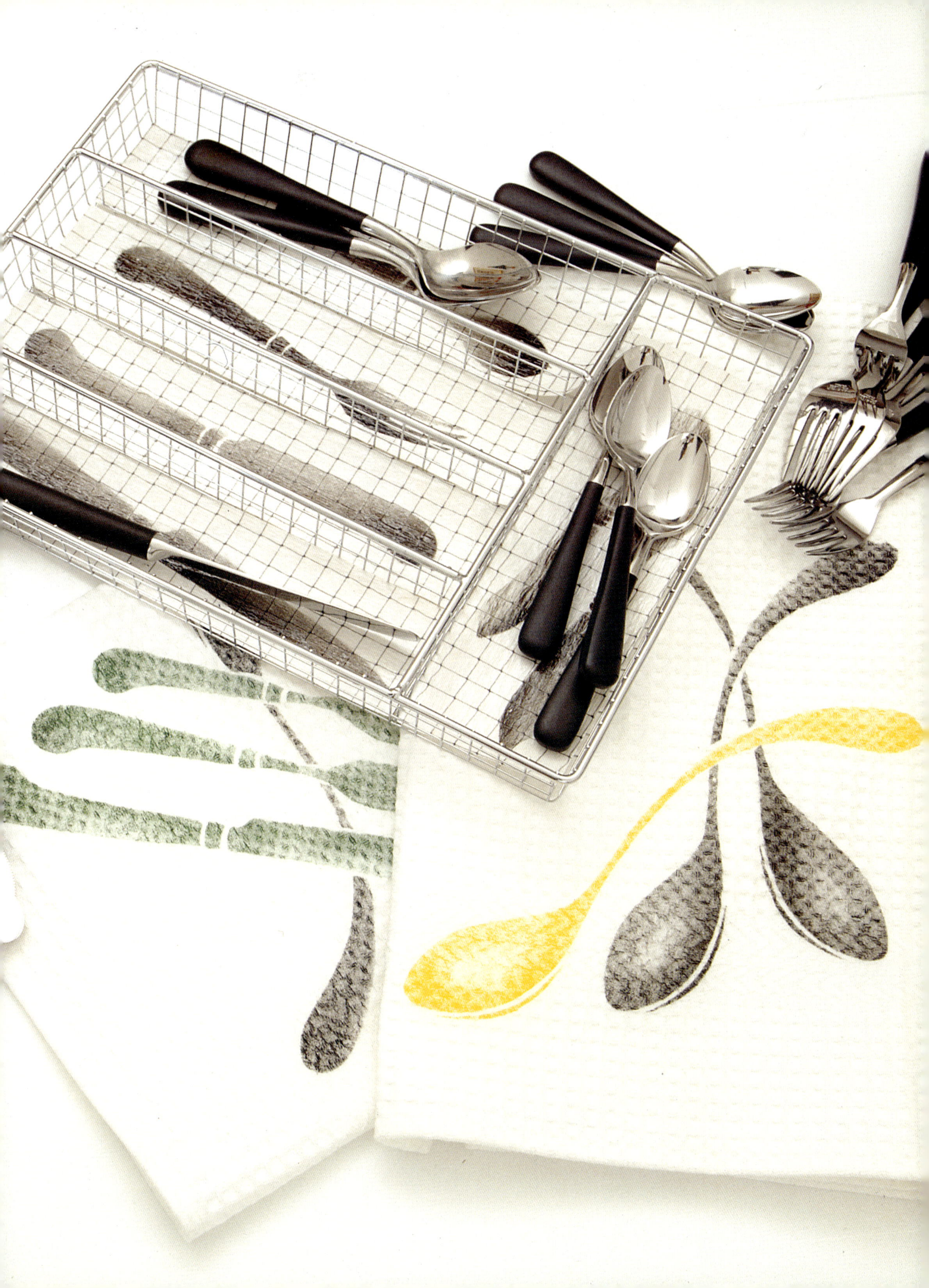

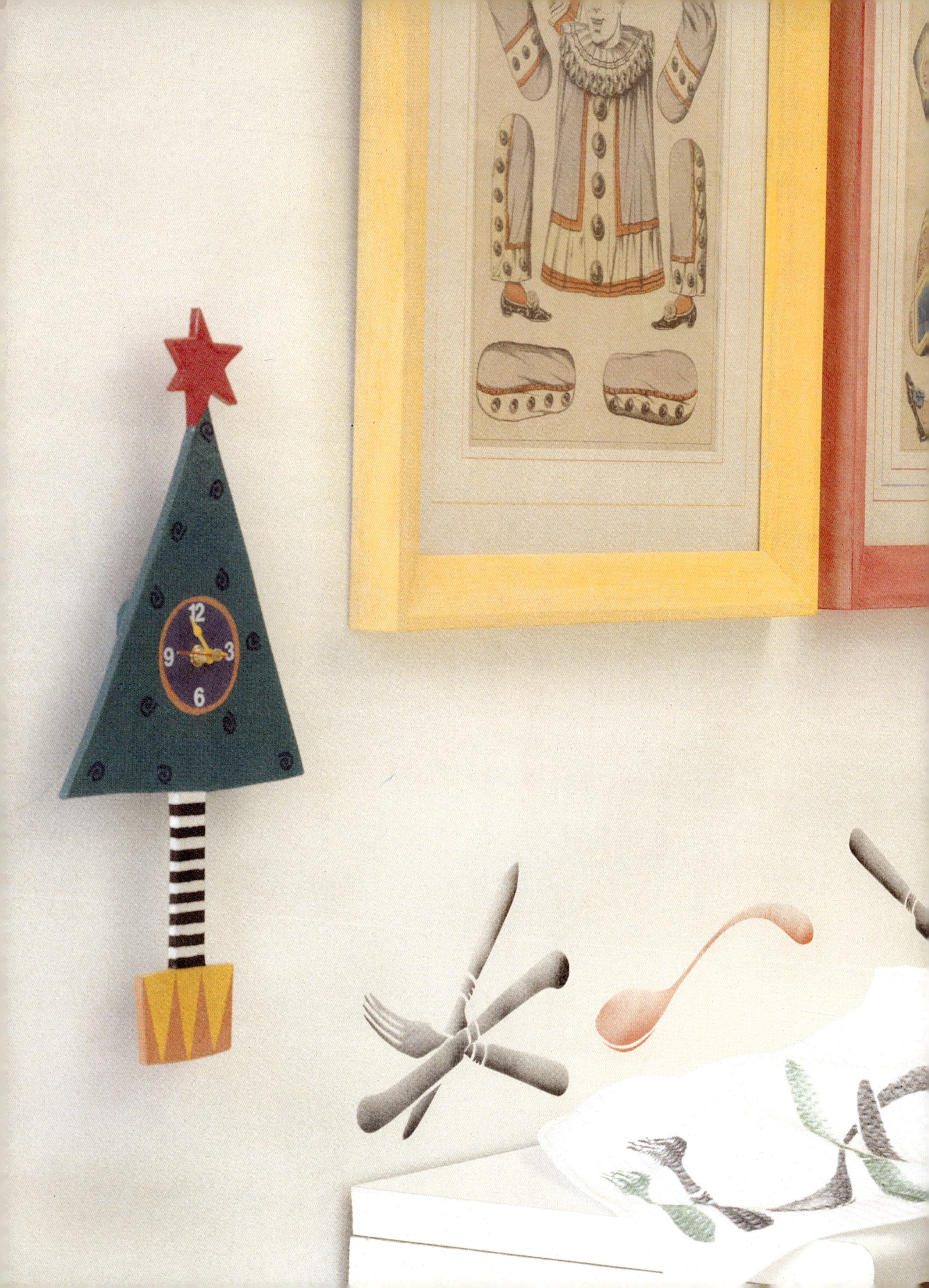

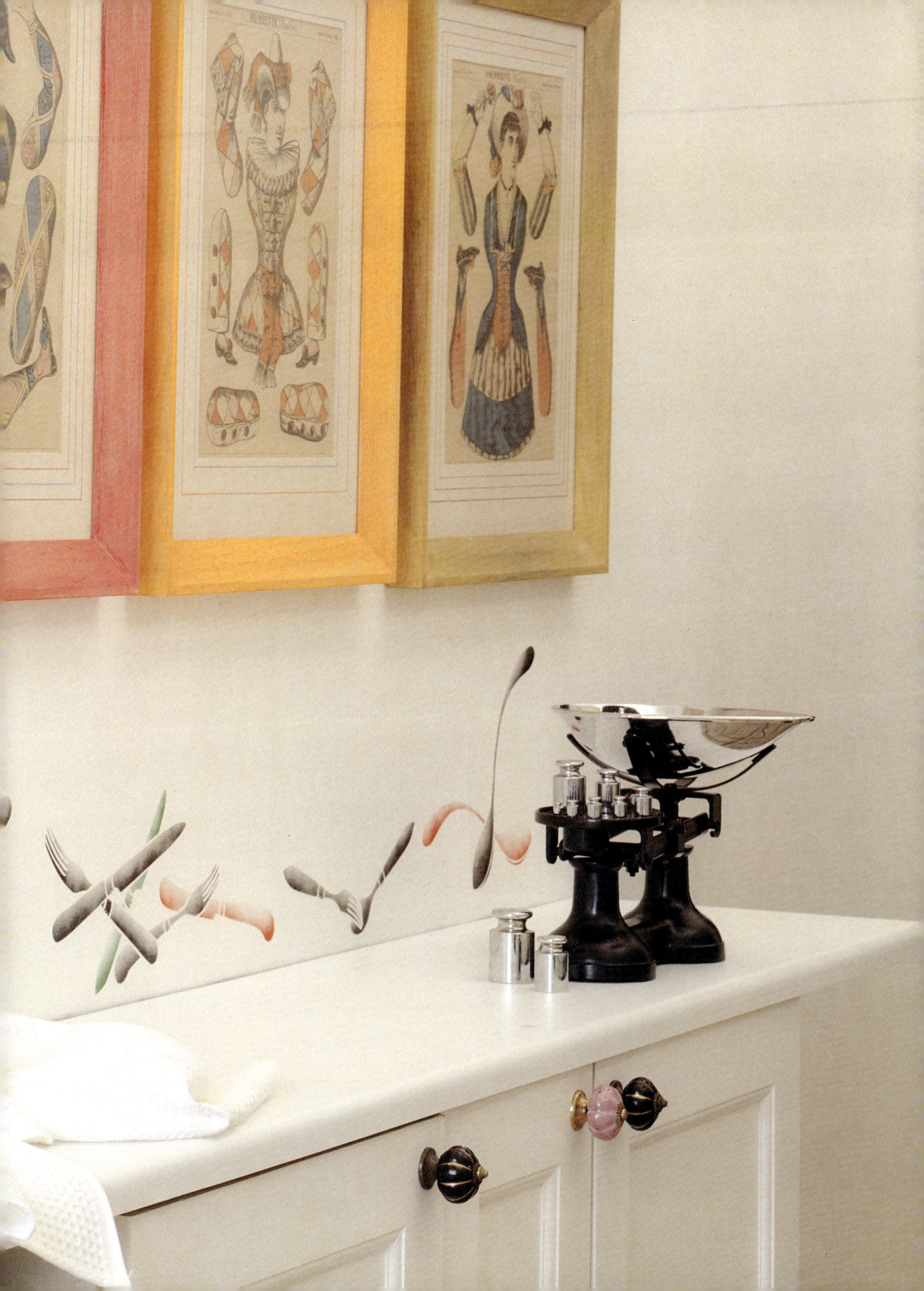

KITCHEN CUTLERY

PLACE MATS

These amusing *trompe l'oeil* place mats were part of my little test before I stencilled the wall. They looked so successful that I made a complete set on thicker paper with a textured surface. Admittedly, the paper place mats would not last very long, but the same idea could just as easily be used on fabric. Instead of stencilling onto separate place mats, you might think about stencilling place settings onto a tablecloth made from white sheeting. To take the idea one step further, you could design your own 'table mats' and stencil them onto the cloth, too, sitting between the cutlery. Use fabric paints and fix them in place by ironing onto the back of the cloth with a suitably hot iron and then you will be able to wash the cloth over and over again without fear of losing all your hard work.

Stencils are incredibly versatile and by changing its size and colour, a single design can provide you with endless variety. Look out for interesting papers, as worn covers to cookery books can be recovered and have neatly stencilled bindings, or make cutlery stencils into book marks for favourite recipes.

Stencil the piece of cutlery of your choice onto some card – white or coloured – and then cover with clear plastic to protect it. Make recipe books as presents by covering a plain paper pad with a smart cutlery stencilled cover, or reduce the cutlery stencil and use the stencil on invitations or menu cards. The stencilled kitchen is not only one that features stencils on its walls, cupboards and curtains – search out those smaller items that can be transformed with the aid of a stencil, some appropriate paint and a paintbrush

---

YOU WILL NEED

Kitchen cutlery stencil
(see pages 66-7)

Sheet mat acetate or
oiled manilla paper

Tracing paper (optional)

Soft pencil (optional)

Cutting mat

Masking tape

Craft knife or small embroidery
scissors

Repositionable spray glue (optional)

Fabric and/or acrylic paints

Stencil brushes

---

1 Before you start stencilling, gather together all your equipment so that you know you have everything to hand. Check that you have the right kind of paints for the surface you intend stencilling on to (see the chart on page 11).

2 Trace the cutlery stencils of your choice from pages 66-7 directly onto mat acetate. However, if you are using oiled manilla paper, trace the cutlery onto tracing paper first and then transfer these outlines onto the oiled manilla paper. To transfer the outlines, draw over the outlines on the back of the tracing paper with a very soft pencil, position the tracing paper on the oiled manilla paper and go over the outlines one more time.

3 Fix the acetate or manilla paper to the cutting board or mat using strips of masking tape. Then draw the blade of the craft knife gently towards you ensuring your supporting hand is away from the blade. For further information on cutting out stencils see step 2 on page 14.

4 Fix the stencil to the surface to be stencilled using masking tape or low-tack repositionable spray glue (see step 3 on page 15). Make sure it is straight and, if important, centred.

5 Apply the paint – see step 4 on page 15 for more help with the stippling technique. To create a truly professional finish, try shading your stencils to give depth, and shade colours into each other for a subtle effect.

SEE ALSO

Sizing a stencil (page 20)

Adapting a stencil (page 21)

Using spray paint (page 29)

These fake place mats are a witty addition to any kitchen table setting.

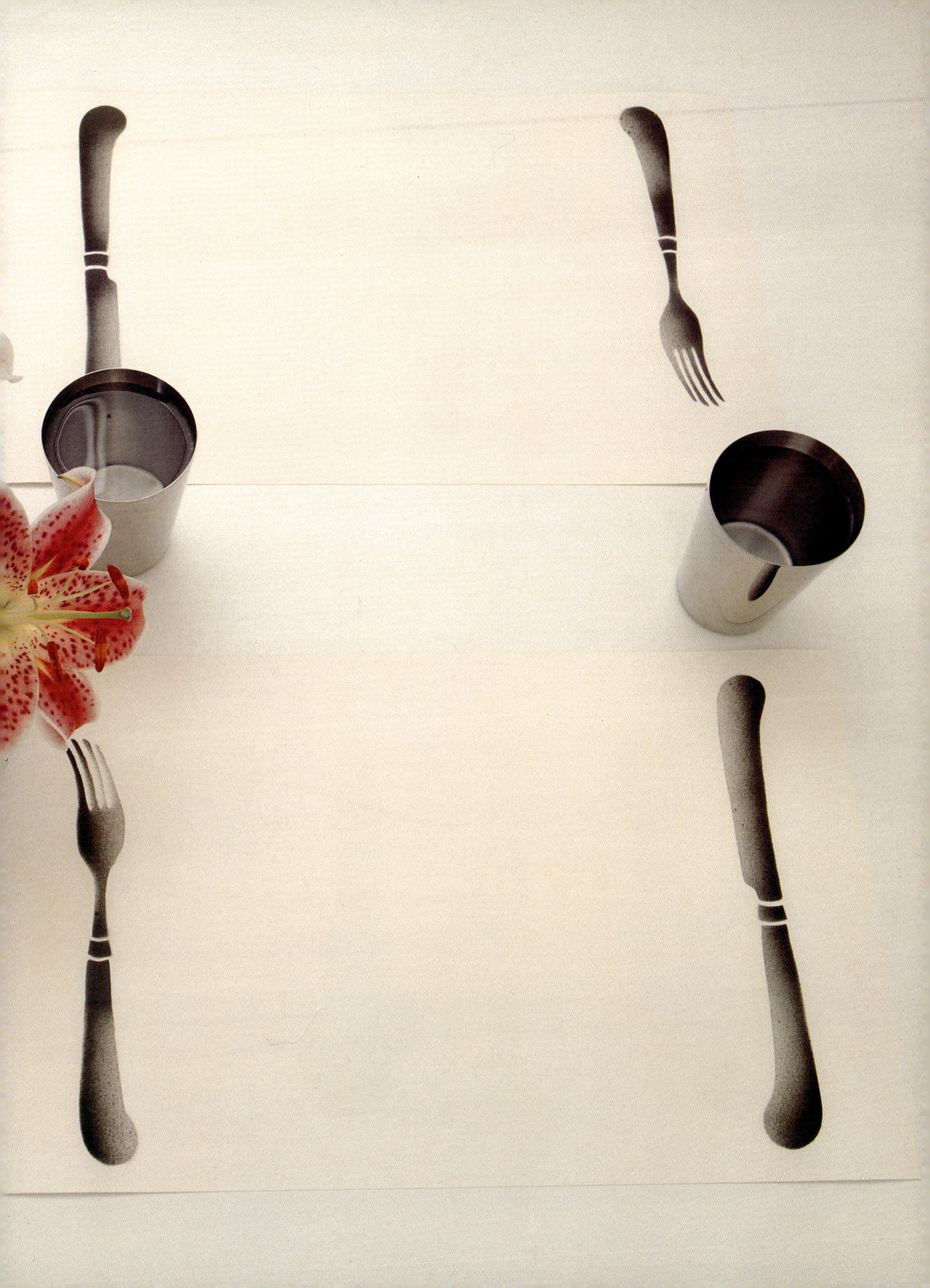

KITCHEN CUTLERY

These kitchen cutlery stencils are ready to be traced directly onto acetate or transferred to oiled manilla paper as described on pages 14 and 21.

KITCHEN CUTLERY

DELFTWARE TILES

Delft is an old city founded in 1075 in the Netherlands just south of the Hague and the famous hand-painted blue and white ceramics that are known as Delftware have been produced since 1653. Delft is located on the Schie River and the city is criss-crossed by canals, so the china artists only had to look out of their windows to be inspired by scenes of boats, barges, sails and the odd windmill.

Over the years, the Delftware designs have retained their charm and fresh, delicate application, influenced most noticeably by Chinese designs, often with pavilions and pagodas introduced next to a windmill, and I have found them quite inspirational. I chose these particular designs as I love to sail and the smaller the boat the happier I am. So with these tiles before me my imagination can sail away as I wash up, prepare food, or take a break for coffee, dreaming of fishing or punting a boat.

The tile designs enliven any plain tiled surface, and with the use of spray paint or ceramic paints they are easily applied. For a sense of consistency, I have repeated just the fine, swirling frame that appears on each design. The scenes may vary within each one, but the edges remain the same.

The use of alternating stencils is demonstrated on the drawn blind overleaf. By covering one of the picturesque designs with masking tape, just the curly corners of each frame can be stencilled, creating an overall tiled pattern on the blind. To lighten the overall effect, I placed the heavier pictorial designs only in the bottom four rows of tiles, and just the swirls are used above. I also decided to alternate a patterned tile with a plain tile so that the translucence of the blind would not be detracted from too much. With the light filtering through it, the blind has just the quality of light and pattern that I was looking for.

Opposite: *By randomly placing the different stencil designs across the wall of this kitchen, a freeflowing pattern is created, reflecting the soft appeal of Delftware tile design.*

Overleaf: *For hot summer days, a blind made from subtly stencilled white cotton is just the thing to keep a kitchen cool and shady.*

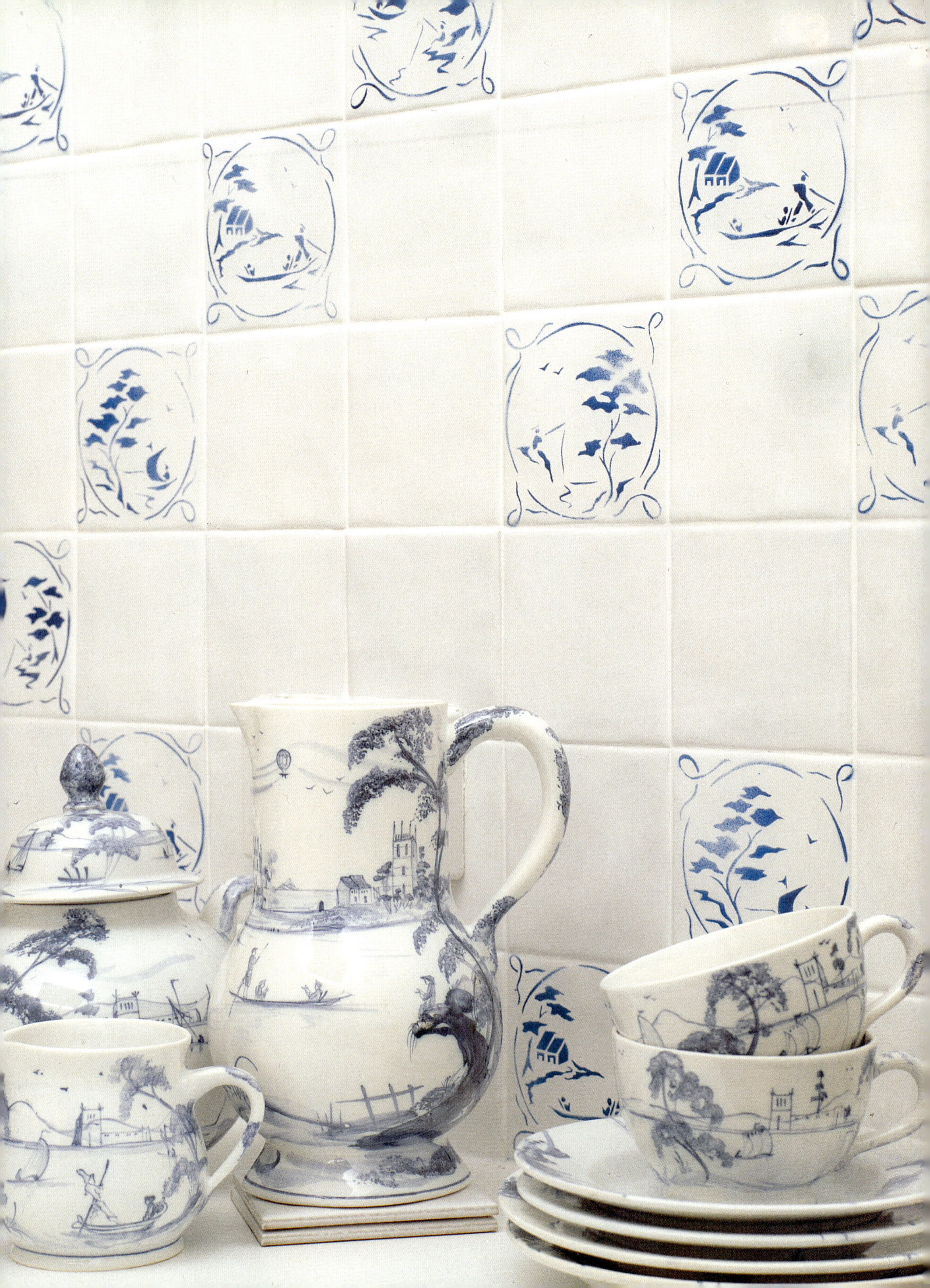

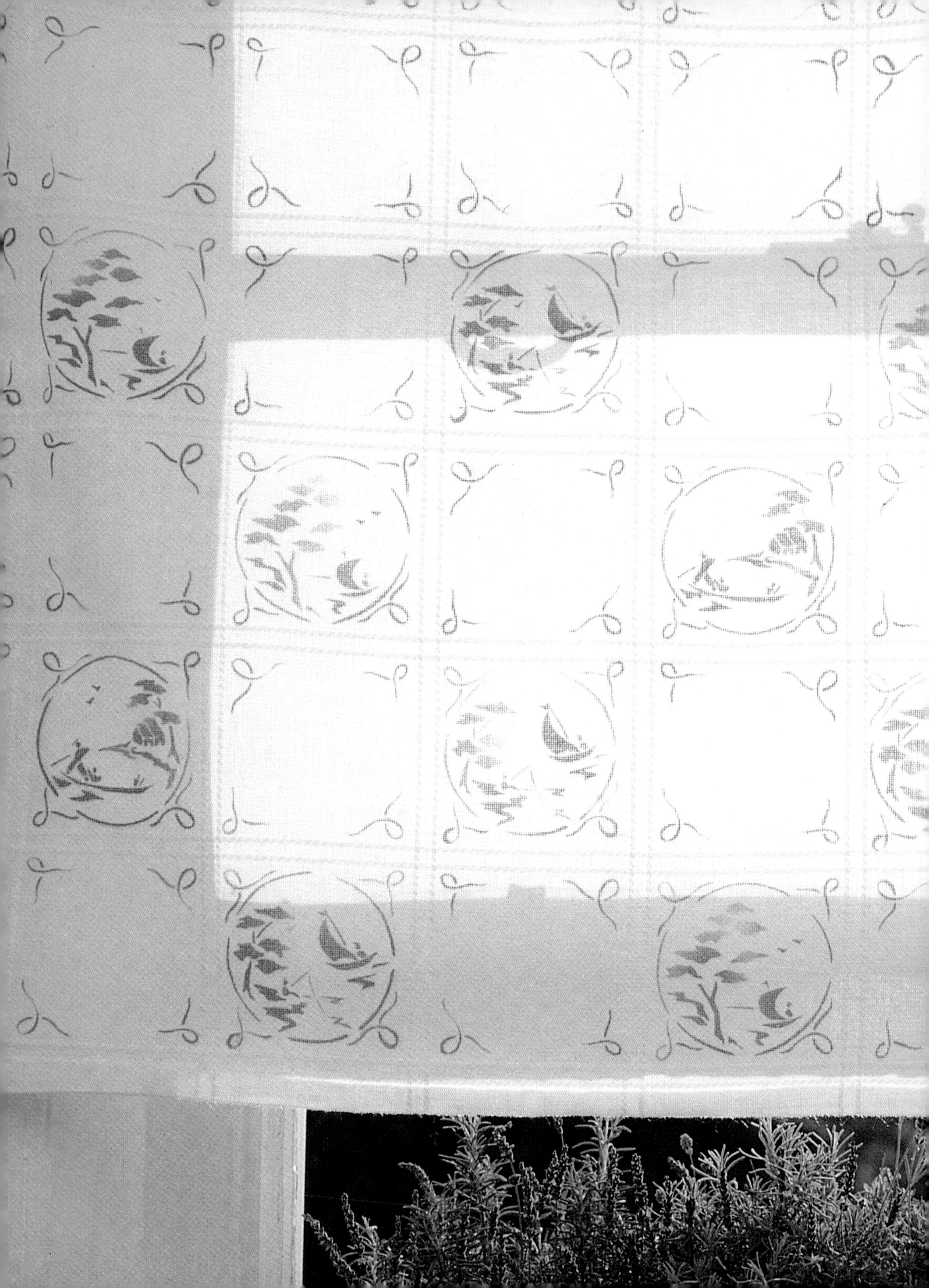

DELFTWARE TILES

TILES ONTO TILES

As my Delftware tile design is square I have deliberately found fabrics with squares interwoven into them to accessorize this kitchen. I then stencilled them with the decorative tiles alone, and also used small parts of each stencil instead of using the whole one each time. Pick out elements to create your own pastoral scene; a family sitting fishing under a tree, or – as in my family's case – racing dinghies across the bay. You will notice in the photograph opposite that I have also used the twisting corner motif to create a border along the edge of the wooden tray.

Many of us inherit the tiles that a previous owner of a house has chosen, and if they are plain they are easy to stencil. If they are patterned or a colour not to your taste, paint over the tiles with concrete floor paint before stencilling. Cold ceramic paints will not last forever but assuming the stencils are not too vigorously cleaned, they will last for a good few years. If you wish to change the stencil on the tiles, however, just wipe away spray paint with nail varnish remover, and ceramic paint with white spirit. But be careful to avoid wiping paint into the porous grouting as it will stain very easily.

Although I have chosen to use blue paint on all the stencilled tiles featured on these pages, don't necessarily feel constricted in the same way. You may feel that your kitchen could use the odd touch of green or red, so stencil some green on a branch or red on a little house. Apply it consistently to each tile, or add a little here and there as your design requires.

YOU WILL NEED

Delftware tiles pull-out stencil (see page 45)

Cutting mat

Masking tape

Craft knife or small embroidery scissors

Repositionable spray glue (optional)

Cold ceramic paints

Stencil brushes

1 Before you start stencilling, gather together all your equipment so that you know you have everything to hand. Check that you have the right kind of paints for the surface you intend stencilling on to (see the chart on page 11).

2 Pull or cut out the stencil from page 45 and then cut it out, fixing the stencil paper to the cutting board or mat using strips of masking tape. Draw the blade of the craft knife gently towards you ensuring your supporting hand is away from the blade. For further information on cutting out stencils see step 2 on page 14.

3 Fix the stencil to the surface to be stencilled using masking tape or low-tack repositionable spray glue (see step 3 on page 15). Make sure it is straight and, if important, centred.

4 Apply the paint – see step 4 on page 15 for more help with the stippling technique. To create a truly professional finish, try shading your stencils to give depth, and shade colours into each other for a subtle effect.

SEE ALSO

Adapting a stencil (page 21)

Using spray paints (page 29)

Smaller elements of the design can be selected as a border, like the twists repeating around the scalloped edge of the tray, individual boats sailing across the tea towel, or the whole design placed over another.

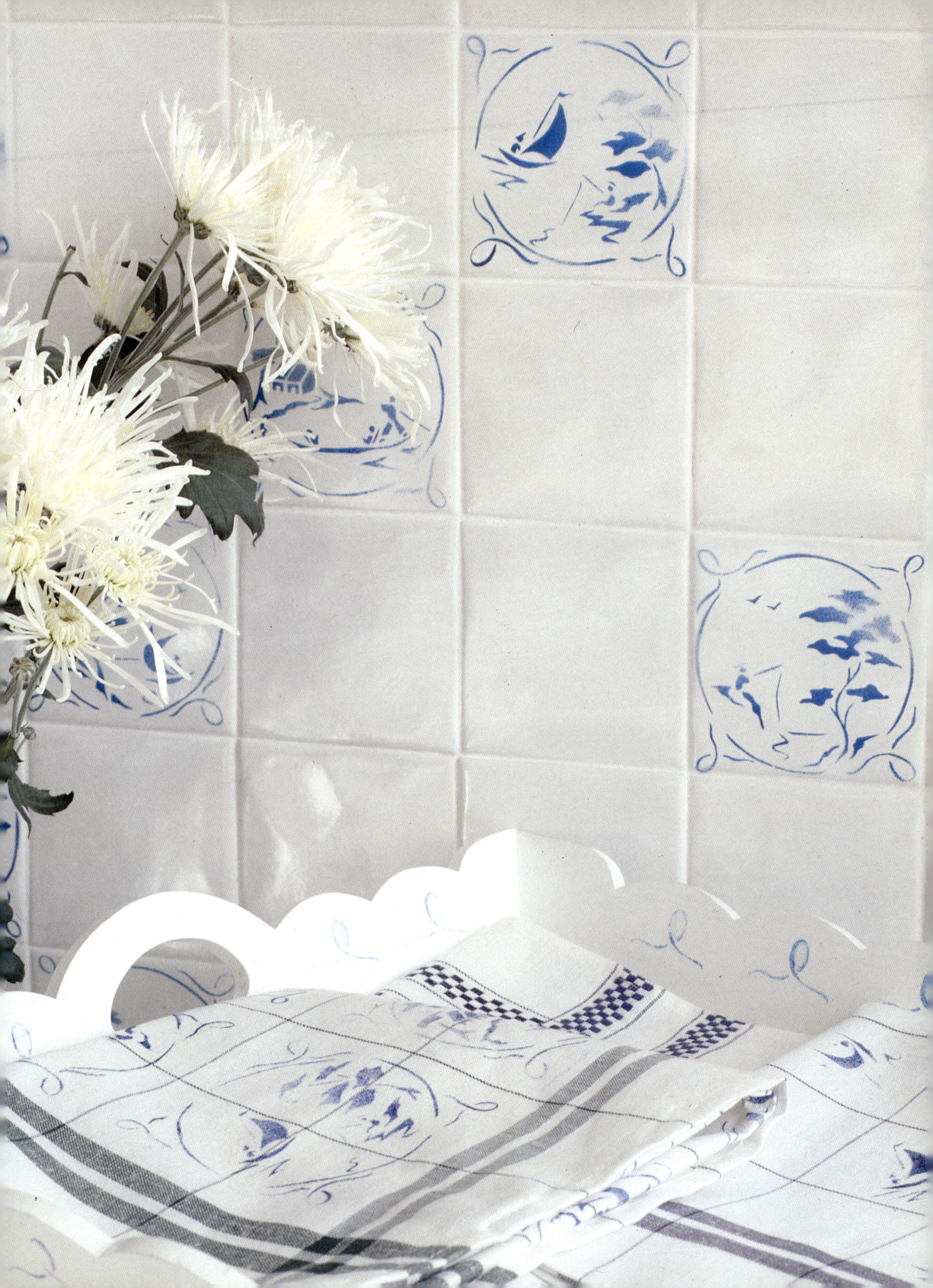

PROVENÇAL SUNFLOWERS

Searching around for a design to stencil onto a parasol, I came across this beautiful fabric from Provence. Its naive design and bright colours were just what I was looking for and by using some of its elements I was able to give my garden chairs and parasol a new lease of life.

To make a stencil that was in the same proportion as the fabric I traced over the fabric and then modified it slightly so that the resulting design would work well as a stencil. The petals on the Provençal design were joined together, but I separated them; likewise, I detached the flower from its stem. To avoid making mistakes as you adapt your designs, shade in each piece that you will eventually be cutting out prior to painting. There are certain rules that are well worth knowing. For example, if you want to stencil a circle, cut two semi-circles with a slight space between each half (if you were to cut a complete circle, the centre would fall out). Also, avoid long straight lines, as the stencil will become wobbly and the lines no longer straight. Instead, incorporate narrow bridges along the line so that the stencil remains firm.

The parasol was a challenge to stencil, not only because of its shape, but also because the fabric had been weatherproofed – and almost stencilproofed, too. Each piece of stippling took a long time to penetrate the weatherproofing. Because the stencil is such an unusual shape, it also took a long time to work out where to position each element. When in doubt, I photocopy a stencil many times and place the cut-out photocopies around the piece to be stencilled, in this case the upturned parasol on the floor. Eventually, I decided that in order to dramatize the movement of the flourish around the edge of the parasol, I would stencil it so that it undulated in and out on each panel (see the photograph overleaf).

Opposite: *It was this Provençal fabric that inspired me to design the stencil featured on the parasol and chairs. Each element is so strong that it made the perfect basis for a stencil.*

Overleaf: *The strong dots that are a feature of the tablecloth's design cluster at the parasol's centre while the sunflowers are stencilled in every other panel. The effect is stunning, and I feel that justice has been given to an exceptional, inspirational fabric.*

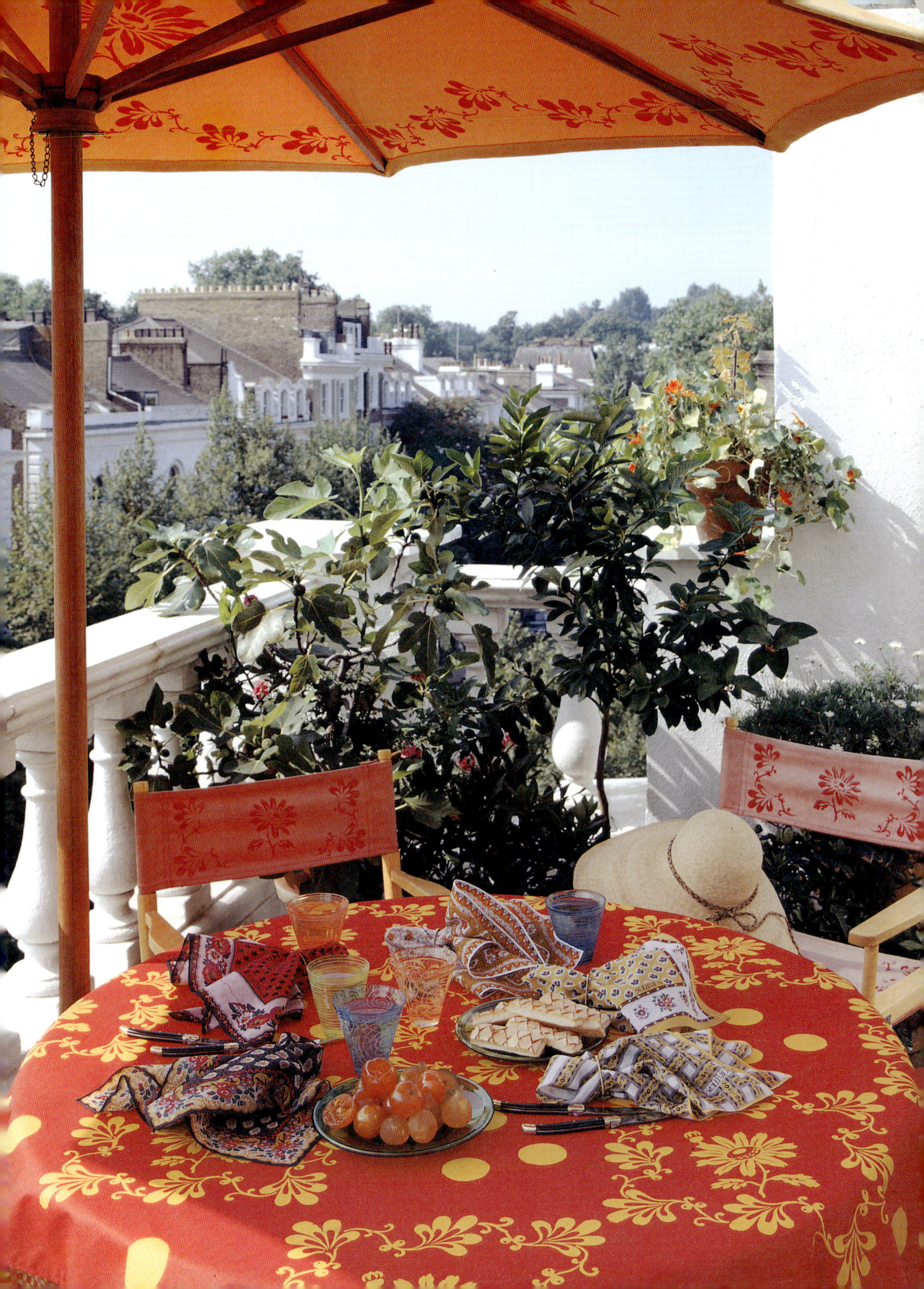

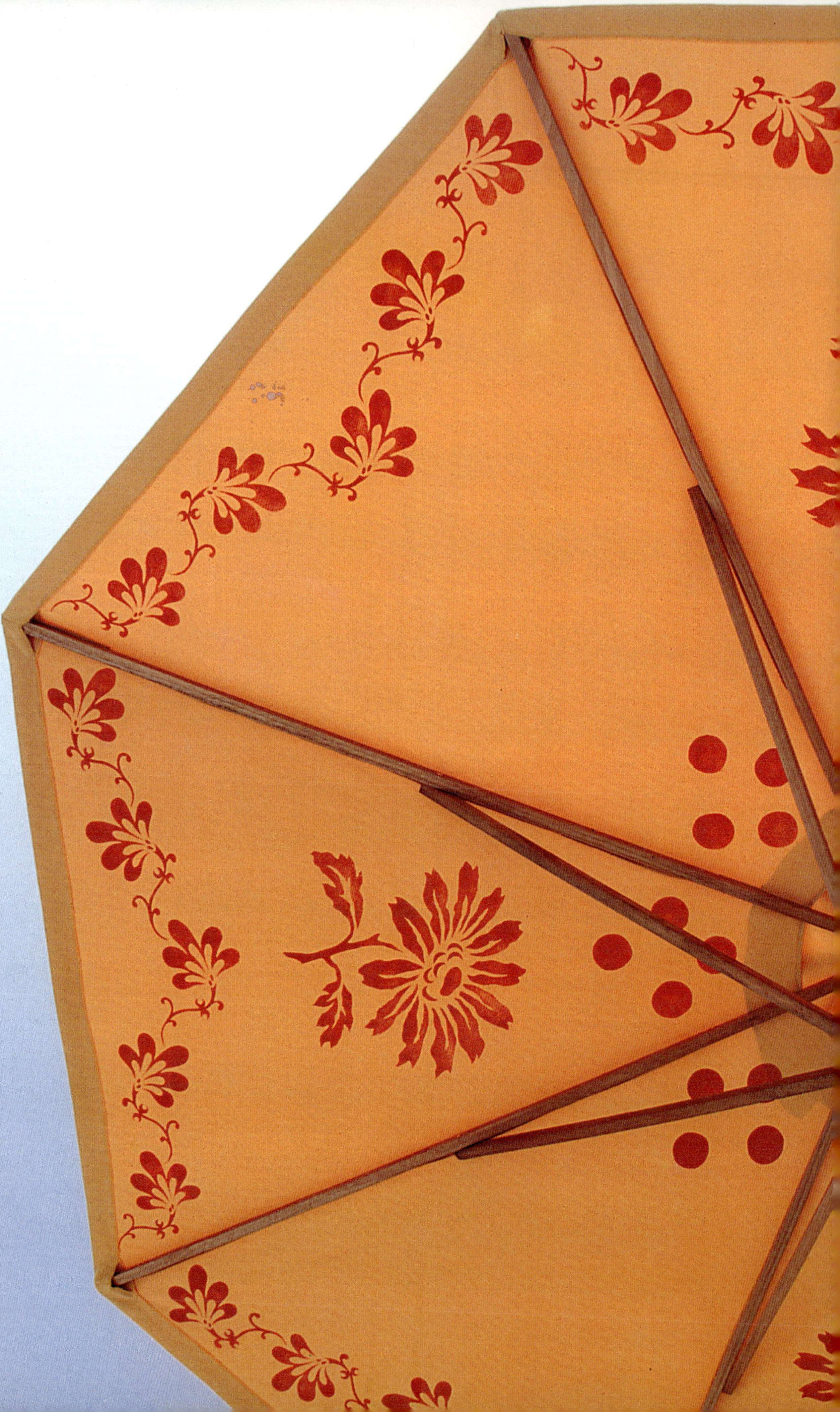

PROVENÇAL SUNFLOWERS

THE CHAIRS

These chairs had seen better days as the canvas had become faded in the sun. However, by using the same crimson fabric paint as on the parasol but with a more delicate application, a faded, aged effect of stencilling was created, designed to complement the canvas. Two elements of the complete stencil have been stencilled onto each chair back as I felt that the solid circles of colour would be too much on a smaller area of canvas like this. The flourish border alone appears on the seats.

YOU WILL NEED

Provençal sunflower pull-out stencil (see page 47)

Cutting mat

Masking tape

Craft knife or small embroidery scissors

Repositionable spray glue (optional)

Fabric paints

Stencil brushes

1 Before you start stencilling, gather together all your equipment so that you know you have everything to hand. Check that you have the right kind of paints for the surface you intend stencilling on to (see the chart on page 11).

2 Pull or cut out the stencil from the centre of this book and then cut it out, fixing the stencil paper to the cutting board or mat using strips of masking tape. Draw the blade of the craft knife gently towards you ensuring your supporting hand is away from the blade. For further information on cutting out stencils see step 2 on page 14.

3 Fix the stencil to the surface to be stencilled using masking tape or low-tack repositionable spray glue (see step 3 on page 15). Make sure it is straight and, if important, centred.

4 Apply the paint – see step 4 on page 15 for more help with the stippling technique. To create a truly professional finish, try shading your stencils to give depth, and shade colours into each other for a subtle effect.

SEE ALSO

Sizing a stencil (page 20)

Adapting a stencil (page 21)

Turning corners (page 28)

Small parts of a stencil can be used to turn corners very simply. If you are not sure how the end result will look, test out your ideas on scrap paper first.

A change of size and colour for the sunflower head has transformed the stencil. Isolating a part of a stencil in this way can be well worthwhile if developing a theme for other parts of the kitchen.

PLACE MATS

To make some stunning place mats, I enlarged the sunflower head alone and stencilled it in brilliant colours. The end result looks totally different, and yet it is still a part of the decorative theme. Thick watercolour or textured papers are excellent to use for mats, and if you intend to use them several times, spray a fixative over the paper to protect the stencil. Small stencilled details could also be used for paper napkins, on papier mâché napkin rings, or temporarily around the outside of glasses or a jug of water.

ACKNOWLEDGMENTS

Daler-Rowney Fine Art and Graphics Material
Daler-Rowney House, Bracknell, Berkshire RG12 8ST.
Tel: 01344 424621 Fax: 01344 486511.
Working with these exceptionally high quality products always gives the best results. The Robert Simmonds stencil brushes come in all sizes are hard wearing and subtle; System 3 acrylic paint is ideal for most stencil work, and the screen printing paint is great for fabric. A full 128-page catalogue demonstrates the diversity of all the products, and gives constructive uses for materials.

DMC Creative World
62 Pullman Road, Wigston, Leicester LE18 2DY.
Tel: 0116 281 1040 Fax: 0116 281 3592.
More than 428 colours to choose from in perle, stranded and sewing cottons, there are also wonderful Zweigart linens, counted weaves and textures. All products are fully washable. There is a comprehensive catalogue and exceptional colour sample charts.

Isis Ceramics
The Old Toffee Factory, 120A Marlborough Road, Oxford OX1 4LS.
Tel: 01865 722729 Fax: 01865 727521.
USA Agent: David Gooding
Tel: 212 570 2254.
My thanks for the loan of their most beautifully hand-painted ceramics featured on page 69. Isis ceramics are distributed throughout the world in distinguished shops.

Jali Shelves
Apsley House, Chartham, Canterbury, Kent CT4 7HT.
Tel: 01227 831710 Fax: 01227 831950.
Jali Home Decoration make decorative trims for shelving, pelmets, brackets, and they also make self-assembly kits. A well-presented catalogue is available, and a mail order service very prompt. The delightful shelves, just a part of the range, are displayed on pages 16-20.

Souleiado Provençal Fabrics
78 Rue de Seine, PARIS, 2, France.
Tel: 33 1 43 54 15 13 Fax: 33 1 43 54 84 45.
There are also many other shops in France and capital cities around the world featuring exquisite collections of Provençal fabrics, both traditional and contemporary designs, in all weights of materials. The Souleiado shops are a feast of fabrics not to be missed. The parasol and chairs on pages 74-9 pick out elements of Souleiado design.